CHRISTOPHER COLUMBUS
and the
AFRIKAN HOLOCAUST

Slavery and the Rise of European Capitalism

A&B PUBLISHERS GROUP
BROOKLYN, NEW YORK

CHRISTOPHER COLUMBUS and the AFRIKAN HOLOCAUST

Slavery and the Rise of European Capitalism

Dr. John Henrik Clarke

Foreword
Dr. Leonard Jeffries

Preface
Dr. Edward Scobie

COVER DESIGN: *A & B PUBLISHERS GROUP*
COVER CONCEPT: *ACT* COMMUNICATIONS GROUP

Library of Congress Cataloging-in-Publication Data

Clarke, John Henrik, 1915 - 1998
    Christopher Columbus and the Afrikan holocaust : slavery & the rise of European capitalism / by John Henrik Clarke..
        p.   cm.
    Includes bibliographical references and index.
    ISBN 1-886433-18-6 $10.95
    1. Columbus, Christopher--Influence. 2. Slave trade--History.
3. Capitalism--Europe--History. 4. Racism--Europe--History.
    I. Title.
E112. C58   1994   94-16193
380. 1'44' 09--dc20   CIP

Published
by

A&B PUBLISHER GROUP
1000 Atlantic Ave
Brooklyn, New York,
11238
(718) 783-7808

02 03 04 05 06 07 08 09   10 9 8 7 6 5 4

Manufactured and Printed in Canada

To Alberta Lewis, a friend of my early days in Harlem, and still a friend in my later years.
This small token of love and appreciation and a reminder that both of us in our own way are part of the African World Liberation Movement.

CONTENTS

FOREWORD

ONCE AGAIN DR. JOHN HENRIK CLARKE has made another out-standing contribution to his school of African knowledge and has furthered the significance of this African-centered perspective on world history. For almost two decades as a distinguished profes-sor of African World History at Hunter College of the City University of New York, and for more than a half a century as a scholar advocate for African peoples, Dr. Clarke has been a bea-con of light in the sea of European-American darkness and blind-ness. He has consistently urged all the people he has come in contact with to seek the truth about human history by pursuing the path of enlightenment through knowledge, first of self and one's people and then others. He has constantly predicted that this path of wisdom would lead to improvement and a new day for Africans everywhere.

As a master teacher Dr. Clarke had always stated clearly that you cannot understand world history without understanding the central role of African history. This short but timely work gives the reader a sense of the urgency of African and world history at this moment in time. The title subject matter of this publication reveals its significance and relevance—Christopher Columbus and the Afrikan Holocaust. Similarly the subtitle is even more po-tent and enlightening—slavery and the rise of European capital-ism. Like many of the African-centered scholars who were Dr. Clarke's teachers and his source of inspiration, he not only gives you accurate analysis and descriptions of history, he provides prescription of what Africans have to do to bring into being a new day.

Dr. Clarke provides an overall analysis of a period of history that has been systematically falsified and hidden from the serious scrutiny of African scholars and researchers and other committed individuals. He points to concepts that are keys to unveiling that truth about African history and destroying the "Big Lies" about White supremacy.

In Professor Clarke's continual quest for African truth, this work is a potent articulation of an all too neglected period of African world history and sets the stage for a more expansive publication that is being prepared by a collectivity of scholars under his able direction, dealing with slavery and its impact on Africa and the world. What are the key concepts articulated by Dr. Clarke? What analytical perspectives does he bring to the history of this period? What historical process does he reveal and scrutinize? What system analysis does he provide the reader and the researcher?

Dr. Clarke challenges the traditional views of African Civilization and its strengths and weaknesses before the enslavement and colonialism periods. He challenges the Eurocentric view of Columbus as a "discoverer" and states that he set in motion the genocidal process and renewed western racism.

Professor Clarke points out that Columbus set in motion political forces that established a global system of exploitation. This system has its roots in the Columbus Era and produced European world domination.

The fifty year period from 1482 to 1536 A.D. has special significance for world history. During this period, the European's world was able to synthesize various economic, political and cultural forces and lay the foundation for a global system of power, centered around materialism, capitalism and imperialism. At the heart of the new global system of European-American materialism was super exploitation of the indigenous people of the Western hemisphere and the enslavement of Africans.

As a result, two worlds collided and left us with a legacy of genocidal institutionalized White supremacy. African and Native American humanism lost out to the system of European materialism.

10

The seeds of the European-American system of materialism were planted during this definitive period of history from 1482– 1536 A.D. and were nurtured by the exploitation of new lands, labor and resources. The centerpiece of this exploitative system was the trans-Atlantic slave trade. This development of Europe and its colonization of the New World or Western Hemisphere goes hand in hand with the underdevelopment of Africa and the indigenous people of the Americas. This thesis was presented by the heroic African scholar from Guyana Dr. Walter Rodney in his classic work *How Europe Underdeveloped Africa*.

The process of African underdevelopment was part of a larger interplay of accidents of history that produced genocidal processes that culminated in the African Holocaust of Enslavement. These historical events connected the growing economic and political forces that laid the foundation of the modern European-American nation state and nationalism as well as the global world economy centered around intercontinental trade and capitalism. This connection between various economic forces institutionalized trade and control over lands, labor and resources on a world scale. The link between capitalism and slavery was forged.

Two monumental works describing and analyzing this period of history and its events were produced by Dr. Eric Williams. His classic work, *Capitalism and Slavery* produced a storm of controversy when it was first published because its thesis linked capitalism with the notorious slave system of dehumanization. These ideas were supported in his later book *From Columbus to Castro*. Dr. Clarke recognized the importance of these works and points out that the system of European-American exploitation which was centered on the enslavement of Africans was initiated by the Catholic nations of Portugal and Spain, but was later dominated by the Protestant British who defeated the Dutch in a series of wars.

This rivalry for control over the Atlantic slave trade system led to wars after wars in Europe, America, Africa and on the high seas. The genocidal process initiated by the Catholic Church and the Catholic nations of Portugal and Spain was taken over by the more efficient and business conscious Protestants of Holland and

England. Dr. Clarke correctly states that the Catholic nations initiated the slavery and genocidal process and were pushed aside as the Protestant Dutch and particularly the English made slavery a system of Big Business, setting the stage for the Industrial Revolution which England initially dominated, in the eighteenth and nineteenth centuries.

Dr. Clarke candidly speaks about the world that Christopher Columbus set in motion that produced war, slavery and genocide over the past five hundred years. Columbus, himself, was a symbol of exploitation and greed and became a role model for later European conquistadors, who raped and pillaged the Americas and Africa. It is ironic that the true story of the Columbus brothers' atrocities against the indigenous American people was preserved and published by a Catholic cleric, Bartolomeo de las Casas, who detailed the murders of the natives in his book on the *History of the Indies*.

The struggle over the legacy of Columbus and the correct history of the African Holocaust of Enslavement is at the heart of the contemporary conflict over the curriculum reform in our schools. Professor Clarke's analysis provides us with a perspective that lets us understand that slavery and genocide were institutionalized and systematized into a global system of domination, destruction and death which not only control land, labor and resources, but colonialized information. All this was done in the name of White supremacy, based upon the concept of "chosen people" and manifest destiny and designed to further cultural genocide and maintain mental slavery. Dr. Clarke's work in the past and his current effort will help to free African minds and allow them to prepare a meaningful future.

DR. LEONARD JEFFRIES
CHAIRMAN AFRICANA STUDIES DEPARTMENT
CITY COLLEGE
NEW YORK

PREFACE

DR. JOHN HENRIK CLARKE'S STUDY ON THE African Holocaust and the devastating effect it wreaked on millions of Africans is most opportune at this time when the Euro-American world is paying homage to Christopher Columbus for his navigational error in 1492, an error which heaped horrors on the Native Americans and Africans in its wake.

Dr. Clarke has examined this colossal dehumanizing of a people with minute detail, step by step, and his chronicle reveals that the African Holocaust was "the greatest single crime in the world" committed against a people. Nothing else can match this massive genocide and destruction.

Dr. Clarke asks in his study why did that have to happen to Africans and replies that "African people have always had and still have something that people want." What he has succeeded in achieving is a monumental definitive work of the most destructive phenomena in the lives of Africans: something from which they are yet to recover fully. That is why he exhorts Africans that they never forget, that there is still much work to be done, and it must be undertaken by each individual person. He stresses that it will call for revolutionary change "to yourself and your community," and he concludes his message in his introduction with these words: "My revolution starts with me and my memorial to the people in the Middle Passage starts right now." It is obvious that this message is addressed to each African individually and must be repeated by everyone.

This examination of the African Holocaust does not concern itself only with the period of time encompassing the hundreds of years of the African slave trade and slavery.

European scholars, be they anthropologist or historian, always seem to confine themselves in their writings about Africans to the fringes of civilization, describing Africans as stunned survivors from this terrible trauma, and not being able to cope with the complexities of civilization. That, as Dr. Clarke shows, is a false portrait. He chronicles the glorious history of Africans before their calamitous meeting with Europeans when the Africans were intellectual giants of the world while Europe was encased in darkness and ice-enclaves. Of this, Dr. Clarke noted, "The Africans have also preserved the intellectual masters of Europe, Plato, Aristotle and Socrates, as well as some of the basics of Christianity. The Europeans would now use that information and turn on the people who preserved it." Africans have not only preserved these European intellectuals but tutored them and were responsible for their historical glory; something for which, scholars like Diop and Obenga stated, credit was never given where it was due. In fact, Africa was treated with total omission and relegated to barbarism while Europe gloried in its sunshine.

That is why it is absolutely crucial that we must reclaim our past glories in order to take our rightful place in the history of the world; a position that puts Africans at the top and first in the beginning of the creating of a world civilization. If Africans fail to do that now, all attempts at a total liberation and empowerment will come to naught. That is the memorial we owe to our ancestors of the Middle Passage. We are the survivors of that journey. Not to take action and make something of their sacrifice will mean that it was all in vain. That can never happen and will never be allowed to happen.

This, then, is the message Dr. John Henrik Clarke leaves with us in his most serious and vital study of "Christopher Columbus and the African Holocaust." Dr. Clarke has not only given us, in his work, a very worthy book. What is of even greater significance to us as Africans is that he has placed us on a life-long sacred mission. Let us then begin on that road.

EDWARD SCOBIE
PROFESSOR EMERITUS
AFRICANA STUDIES DEPARTMENT
CITY COLLEGE
NEW YORK

INTRODUCTION

THE VOYAGES OF COLUMBUS MARK A starting point of world capitalism and the beginning of European colonial domination of the world. That is what the ruling powers want everyone to celebrate.

But it hasn't gone down like that. The oppressed people have a different view. Throughout the past year there have been debates and confrontations whenever the ruling powers have tried to celebrate Columbus and their system—in Spain, the United States and throughout the Western Hemisphere. In the Dominican Republic recently the media reported that soldiers shot into a crowd of anti-Columbus demonstrators and killed at least two people. In Peru, the growing Maoist people's war reveals an important truth: the world system that emerged since Columbus is under assault; its days are numbered.

The proletariat and oppressed peoples have nothing to celebrate on October 12. The Columbus anniversary is a celebration of mass murder, slavery, and conquest. More: it exalts the continuing oppression of billions of people today. Columbus is something only oppressors (or fools) could celebrate.

This article was first published in the *Revolutionary Worker* a year ago. It sketches the true history of this so-called "first encounter".

It is said that the Columbus voyage was the "first encounter" between the "New World and the Old World." This is contrary to all known information.

Travelers from the great African empire of Mali in the 1300s reported that the king of Mali told them of two expeditions with hundreds of boats sent from Africa west into the great ocean. Some evidence suggests that there may have been periods of ancient trade from to Brazil . There is physical evidence of a settlement in dating back to the year 1000. And by the time of Columbus himself, it had become routine for English fishermen to travel across the Atlantic to fish the outer banks where they often caught sight of the mainland to the west.

Altogether the historical record suggests as many as twenty contacts and sightings before Columbus.

Why then is the Columbus voyage considered "first"? Because, for the modern ruling classes, the important point is not the actual contact between peoples—it is the world-historic growth of capitalism in Europe made possible by the plunder of the Americas. And that did not start before Columbus."

The above quotes are selected to illustrate the fact that Christopher Columbus discovered absolutely nothing, that he was an adventurer, an opportunist and a willful murderer and a liar and that what he set in motion was the basis of Western capitalism and exploitation of both Africans and Indigenous Americans who had committed no crimes against European people and did not know of European intention to conquer and enslave them. Both the Africans and the Indigenous Americans befriended the Europeans at first, only to be rewarded by enslavement. They did not protect themselves from the Europeans because they did not believe there was a need to. The literature exposing Christopher Columbus and the protracted crimes he set in motion is massive and still growing. Today former Columbus cheerleaders have discarded the word "discovery" and are now using the word "encounter." They too are aware of the fact that Christopher Columbus discovered absolutely nothing. He was a man of achievement, tragic and dubious though the achievement may be. A capsule summary of Mike Ely's article is as follows:

"The U. S. imperialists love Columbus. They have named cities, counties, towns, rivers, colleges, parks, streets and even their capital after him. And now they are organizing a global celebration. Yet, to the people, the facts are plain: Columbus was a thief, an invader, an organizer of rape of Indian women, a slave trader, a reactionary religious fanatic, and the personal director of a campaign for mass murder of defenseless peoples. The bourgeoisie hides these truths as they insist on celebrating him. They say, "Why can't we celebrate him for his seamanship and his daring?" Columbus was utterly lost when he arrived on the beaches of the Bahamas. Until he died, he swore that he had landed in the eastern shore of Asia (which in reality is half a world away!) On his second voyage, he had his crew sign papers that declared that if they told anyone the island of Cuba was not the mainland of China, he would have their tongues cut out. Any reading of his diaries reveals that he was filled, not with a lofty courage or adventurous curiosity, but only the most extreme craving to plunder and enslave unarmed people. They say, "Why can't we judge Columbus by the standards of his time, not of ours?" This is a revealing argument. We can ask whose "standards" of 1492 is the measuring rod. The Taino people? The African people? The peasant rebels of Spain? Or the conquistadors themselves?

The modern imperialists even adopt a sly "multicultural" cover saying, "Why can't we celebrate all the cultures that come together to make America today? Can't we use this celebration to heal the wounds from the past?" And the answer is that this view refuses to distinguish between oppressor and oppressed—the Spanish conquistador and subjugated Indian are not just two "heritages" to be celebrated. Why should such wounds be "healed" when this celebration glorifies capitalist oppression that continues—when the legacy of that past is stamped on every event and social relationship. "

The controversy around Christopher Columbus, his alleged discovery and what his encounter with the Indigenous Americans set in motion has prompted Pope John Paul III to bring some peace in moderation to the Salvadorians. In a speech in Santo

Domingo he has asked the Indians and the Africans to forgive their captors and their enslavers. The following excerpt is from the *Daily Challenge:*

"SANTO DOMINGO, Dominican Republic-Pope John Paul Tuesday pleaded with all native Indians of the Americas and African Americans to forgive the White man for 500 years of injustices and offenses.

The pope also said there was no doubt European colonizers had inflicted 'enormous suffering' on native Indians because they were not able to see them as children of the same God.
'In the name of Jesus Christ and as pastor of the church, I ask you to forgive those who have offended you,' the pope said in a message to the hemisphere's indigenous peoples.

'Forgive all those who during these 500 years have been the cause of pain and suffering for your ancestors and for yourselves,' the pope said in a nine-page message to Indians.

His message came one day after thousands of Indians throughout the hemisphere marked the 500th anniversary of Christopher Columbus' arrival in America with bitter protests against the European invaders.

African American groups have also boycotted commemorations of Columbus, saying his arrival began the destruction of native cultures and led to the African slave trade.

The pope, however, has praised Columbus, saying his discovery led to the introduction of Christianity in the New World. In distinguishing between colonization and evangelization the pope has condemned past and present injustices against indigenous people while defending the church's work on their behalf over the centuries."

What the pope seems to have forgotten (if he cared to think about it at all) is a concept of Christianity created by Europeans for Europeans and that this Christianity is now a handmaiden of European conquest and expansion throughout the world. Dr. ben-Jochannan has said, "Religion is the deification of a people's culture." By extension I have also added religion is the deification of a people's politics and power intent. I wonder will the pope ever be willing to ask the Jews to forgive the German or European Holocaust? This was a crime committed in Europe by Europeans against European people. In size and scope it was small in comparison to the great holocausts in history. The holocausts against the African Americans and the Indigenous Americans mistakenly called Indians was more than a hundred times worse than the European Holocaust that we know so much about. Father Lawrence Lucas, who belongs to the same church as the pope, has reminded us that before there can be forgiveness there must first be repentance. Has the pope called on the criminals who destroyed and enslaved African Americans and Indigenous Americans in the millions to repent? Once he calls on them to repent I believe that some of us will consider forgiving some of them. Until there is some show of repentance on the part of our enemy we will wear our desire for revenge like a badge of honor.

The pope concludes his message in the following manner:

On the last full day of his trip to the Dominican Republic, the pope met separately with representatives of Indians and African Americans in the Vatican's embassy here and gave them two written messages for all their peoples throughout the Americas.

In his message to Indians of all tribes, the pope said the church could not forget the "enormous sufferings inflicted on the people of this continent during the era of conquest and colonization."

He said the abuses committed by the European Christian colonizers were due to the "lack of love in those people who were unable to see the indigenous as brothers and sons of the same God."

In a separate message to African Americans he condemned as a "shameful trade" the African slavery which followed the discovery of the New World and said the Christians responsible had betrayed their faith.

The pope again defended the work of early missionaries from the accusations that they were partners in colonization as the cross and the sword marched together. "What other motives if not preaching the ideas of the gospel spurred the missionaries to denounce the injustices committed against the Indians at the time of the conquest? " he asked.

He assured them the church was well aware of "the alienation that weighs on you, the injustices you suffer, the serious difficulties you have in defending your lands and your rights, the frequent lack of respect for your customs and traditions."

He promised them that the church would raise its voice in condemnation whenever their human dignity was violated.

In his message to African Americans the pope denounced the "very grave injustice committed against the Black populations of the African continent, who were violently uprooted from their lands, their culture and their traditions and taken as slaves to America."

He called the slave trade "an enormous crime" and "an ignoble commerce."

"These men and women were victims of a shameful trade, which was carried out by people who were baptized but did not live according to the principles of their faith," he said:

"How can one forget the enormous sufferings inflicted on populations deported from the African continent, in contempt of the most basic human rights?"

"How can one forget the human lives cut down by slavery? There is a need to confess, in all truth and humility, this sin of man against man," the pope said.

The pope said he was addressing his message to Indians of all tribes from Alaska to the Tierra del Fuego at the southern tip of South America.

Like most religious people, the pope is idealistic but not realistic. I think he would benefit from reading Father de las Casas' books, *The Disruption of the Indies* and *The Tears of the Indians*. I would also refer him to Eric Williams'*From Columbus to Castro* and *Documents on West Indian History*. After reading these books, he might understand why most of us, both African Americans and Indigenous Americans lack the capacity to "forgive" or forget the monumental crimes committed against our people.

In this short book I am referring to what Christopher Columbus set in motion. In his period, he set in motion an act of criminality that influences our very life today. He laid the basis for western racism, misconceptions about people and extensive use of organized religions as a rationale for the enslavement of people. It's a reoccurring event in history and it told us—as nothing has told us before—that history is never old, everything that ever happened continues to happen. What we are dealing with now is more than the second rise of Europe we're dealing with the rise of a concept that has taken hold of the mind of most of the world. People throughout the world are now fighting to get away from that concept and most of the world are now prisoners to that concept.

We're dealing with the reason certain things looked as though they were going to succeed and did not succeed. We're actually dealing with the reason the African Independence Explosion did not culminate in independence for Caribbean states, it achieved independence in name only, " flag independence." However in terms of actual economic independence they are more dependent now than they were at the height of colonialism. It set in motion the exposure of the fact that once you are oppressed and once certain information is kept from you, you begin to experience some confusion about what independence consists of. The African Holocaust that Christopher Columbus helped set in motion is both historical and current. We need to carefully examine its initial impact in order to understand its reverberations. There is a need to look at the world before Columbus. Let's examine the world of Columbus' day and look at his impact on the Americas. Let's look at the world he did not discover. What he actually did—and he should be credited for this—he set in motion the exploitation of two continents for European domination. He never set foot on North America or South America. He set in motion an attitude that is still with us; a concept called "divine/White right and something else called "manifest destiny."

The assumption was—because European had the ships and the basic technology—they had the right to go into other people's country and exploit their mineral resources, take their women and rape them at will. They did all of this in the name of a God that they said was merciful and kind. All of them, including the Arabs, used western-oriented religions...which made their God ungodly.

Now, the role of religions in the domination and destruction of African civilizations was ruthless. There is no exception; Islam was as guilty as all the rest of them. The role of religion in this matter is so shameful that no matter how you look at it, the picture is negative. All of them did more harm than good.

Now let's look at the world from 1400 to 1600 before they come to what is called the New World which was not "new" at all. During the Crusades the Europeans had exploited each other to the point where Europe was about to explode within itself. The Catholic church in its need for funds to build these massive cathedrals and to support parasitic priests had begun to fleece the people to the point where the faithful began to have some serious questions about the role of the Church. The Church in its desire to get still more money from the people, created something called purgatory. Now when you died you didn't go directly to heaven you went to purgatory. Your family and friends had to ransom you from purgatory. The more money you gave the priest the harder and quicker he prayed to get grandma and uncle from purgatory into heaven.

It was a religious con game played on the people of Europe. They were beginning to discover this game to a point and, out of anger, Europe was about to explode within itself. Then a fortunate incident would happen. An off-beat, beatnik, hermit named

Peter came across Europe saying that the infidel Arabs were barring Europeans from visiting the Holy places, observing the Holy Grail and visiting the place of the Crucifixion. Michael Bradley in his book, *Holy Grail Across the Atlantic*, has proven that there was no Holy Grail in the first place and it wasn't lost in the second place and it wasn't where they thought it was in the third place. The pope saw a reason he could use to cut down on all of this anger against the Church. The propaganda swept through Europe that they had to move across Europe in a crusade to rescue this mythological Holy Grail that wasn't lost in the first place. Now they started to march, moving across Europe, to the rescue. However, in the movement across Europe, they forgot the pent-up anger against the Church. This gave the Church a new lease on life which would last until the rise of Martin Luther who would then challenge the Church again and lay the basis of Protestant Reformation. There were many crusades and many reasons for people going on crusades, none of which had anything to do with religion or God.

The way the story is presented to you in school, you think it has something to do with holiness. It has something to do with European power and Europe rising from the Dark Ages; it has something to do with Europe's search for something outside of Europe to eat; something to do with European emotionalism venting itself on people outside of Europe and something to do with Europe trying to find a scapegoat for its own anger. Europe was trying to deflect the fact of its own enslavement of other Europeans. They would call it feudalism but it was an enslavement. It was European enslavement of other Europeans.

The Crusaders won all the battles in Cecil B. De Mille's movies; he gave them victories, but, in many cases, in real history, they got the hell beaten out of them. These well-dressed lords took with them common/ordinary people to do their work and their laundry...these common/ordinary people saw these lords with their tails being beaten and on their knees begging for mercy before the alleged "infidel" Arabs. They began to understand that these men who owned land and controlled their lives were less than God. In the meantime back in Europe, some of the young lords had given up a privilege that the old lords were hanging onto, the privilege of first night.

If you lived on the lord's land and you married, he had the privilege of spending the first night with your wife. Some of the young lords had conceded that the poor critter should at least have that privilege. Now when the old lords came back into Europe there was a semblance of human recognition for the serf (the White slave) on the plantation. This semblance of human recognition would lead to more demands. It would lead to a fight against child labor. While it didn't lead to the banishment of prostitution it would lead to workhouses and places where they could at least put people out of sight.

Europe had lost one-third of its population through famine and plagues. On the eve of 1400 AD, this is the sight you see in Europe...far less in creature comforts than anything in Africa and Asia. They were engaged in tribal warfare in Europe as they are engaged in genocidal conflict right now...only in Europe you don't call it tribal warfare. You will not deal with the fact that not only what is happening in Russia today is tribal warfare it is partly race war.

You forgot the millions of Asians who went into Europe and didn't go home. Asian men who came without women and didn't go home to satisfy that biological necessity. Indeed, if it is a necessity all the time...that's another lecture. I think we've overdone that assumption. What is always a biological pleasure is not always a biological necessity. Let's at least concede that much.)

These Europeans intermingled with these Asians to create a European ethnic entity that is still in Europe. Europe was still hungry and awakening. While it was awakening, it began to pay some attention to the new light in Europe, Spain. Spain was then dominated by Africans, Arabs and Berbers. This combination of Africans, Arabs, Berbers and Jewish financial managers known as Grandees were totally in control of Spain, parts of France and Portugal where the Africans and Arabs had lost power in 1240 AD. However, in 1415 the Portuguese got up enough nerve to attack a small place on the coast of Northwest Africa (present-day Morocco). It was a place called Ceuta. As battles go, it wasn't much of a battle, and as places go it wasn't much of a place. I've visited the place and some say it's about the size of Central Park. I've walked all over it; it's not as big as Central Park. The Battle of Ceuta was a turning point. After 711 A.D. when Jebel Tarik, an African general, or Tarikh ben Zaid, led an army into Spain. Spain had been under the domination of Africans, Berbers, and Arabs. Europe had lived in fear of what they referred to as the "infidel" Arabs in the Mediterranean. Europe, being blocked from the trade in the Mediterranean cringed and it was the Arab that drove this European into the so-called Middle Ages by destroying the European market in the Mediterranean. The Battle of Ceuta asserted the European and subsequently they began to claim access to the Mediterranean. By 1455, arguments between the Arab and the African over puritanical approaches to women and Islam had weakened the African/Arab hold on Spain in the Mediterranean.

When the African joins a religion, he is a puritan within that religion. Other people join a religion and use it for their best interests. But when the African joins it, he takes it for its purest form. I have said before that we African people will out-Pope the Pope and we out-Mohamet Mohamet in matters pertaining to both religion and political ideology.

Spain and Portugal would now approach the pope and the pope would say to them, "You two good Catholic nations stop fighting among yourselves. You are both authorized to reduce to servitude all infidel people." You should read Eric Williams' *Capitalism and Slavery* . A lot of people think it's an old chestnut. This book written over forty years ago, is still current and relevant in its information. Brion David, a scholar at Cornell University wrote a book called *Slavery and Western Civilization*. That book is three times larger and says less. The forgotten character has not been taken into consideration—I'm still on my way to Christopher Columbus--Prince Henry the Navigator. Prince Henry got hold of a cache of maps which were mostly made by Jewish gold dealers who had been dealing in the Western Sudan and the coast of West Africa. The Western Sudan is comprised of the nations in Inner West Africa as opposed to the coastal nations of West Africa. Europe is beginning to see the shape of certain parts of Africa; they are no longer guessing on all of it. Prince Henry, now with these maps, begins to open up a school for chart-making and map-making to let the European know something about the other parts of the world.

I recently appraised a book that called Prince Henry the initiator of the slave trade...which is inaccurate. He did set European maritime skills in motion. Using the maritime information the Africans and the Arabs had preserved at the University of Salamanca [Spain], Europe would now go back to sea; it had previously forgotten longitude and latitude. In other words, when they put a ship out to sea, they wouldn't know which way to turn it; they didn't know east from west.

That challenge from Mediterranean Africans the challenge of the Moors, that challenge of the Arabs had driven Europe into the Middle Ages and had dulled the senses of Europe to the fact that they lived now in fear. Prince Henry—while called the Navigator—didn't navigate anything and there is no evidence that he ever went to sea. The main thing Prince Henry did was to introduce Europe to maritime information. The European in turn used the maritime information coming out of China (then the leading maritime nation of the world) to go out to sea again and to get rid of some of the old wives' tales about the sea. Some of the tales were that if you go so far the sea drops off; the world was flat, not round.

The European had begun to make up his mind...all the hunger, all the famine now...that he had ships and guns, the European didn't care what shape the world was in. Round or flat. He wants it all. Round or flat. Sometimes African people approach European power brokers with the assumption that Europeans are going to give us back things that they had already taken from us. They took it from you; you've got to take it back.

There is some indication that a little-known sailor, Cristobal Colon (Christopher Columbus) attended one of Prince Henry's schools of chart-making. There he learned the basis of maritime skills. We have no evidence that he had, or ever had, any command. This gets us into a mystery about Columbus.

Michael Bradley, in a new work called *The Columbus Conspiracy*, found so much dirt under the name Columbus...he maintains that there were two Columbus's. No one man could have been capable of that much dirt according to Bradley. This includes seven illegitimate children. When he is faced with the different children that were born and the women, he couldn't have moved that fast from one to the other. If he sired one over here, he couldn't have gotten to another place fast enough to bring another one into the world. We have to deal with another date neglected in history, 1482. Ships land off the coast of what is now Ghana, earlier the Gold Coast. They insist now on building permanent fortifications. Portuguese ships had been coming along that coast since 1438. They would take a few slaves out of the country (1442). The Portuguese king, seeing Africans so well dressed and seeing them bringing presents, assumed that they were visiting royalty and in turn gave them presents and sent them home; the idea of enslavement had not reached his mind.

The important thing about this trip when they forced their way into Ghana and an African King, King Ansa, differed with them and told them, "If we saw each other infrequently, maybe we could maintain our friendship. Too much familiarity would erode our friendship." He was beginning to see what could happen. Then in the beautiful last lines of his speech he said, "The sea is forever pushing against the land and the land with equal obstinance is forever pushing against the sea." He understood what could happen. But those Portuguese who could not sell him the Bible-story, forced that gun-story on him. They forced their way in and they built Elmina Castle, the first of the great slave forts along the coast of Ghana. If 36 of the 42 slave fortresses are in Ghana, this tells you that Ghana was the headquarters of the slave trade. I mention this because there is some evidence to indicate that Christopher Columbus was a part of this expedition. He says in his diary, "As man and boy, I sailed up and down the Guinea Coast for twenty-three years." What was he doing up and down the coast of West Africa for twenty-three years? He was in the early Portuguese slave trade. This is Christopher Columbus. Now let's go to 1492.

In 1492 things happened other than the alleged "discovery" that was not a discovery at all. Let's deal with two African events that helped to set certain things in motion. In 1492 Spain was whitening up through the marriage of Queen Isabella and King

Ferdinand. They began now to expel the Moors, the Africans and the Arabs. If they expelled the Jews—and they did—that means that they did not consider the Jews to be White.

Most of the Jews were Sephardic. The same descendants of these Sephardic Jews are second-class citizens in Israel right now...though they are the majority of the population. Not a single field officer in the Israeli army is a Sephardic, even though they are the majority in the army. That army is dominated by Whites and the same is true of the Russian Army. You've got millions of Asians in Russia. I'm showing you the white face is white. Left or right, no matter what they say they believe, religiously or politically they play the race game. You have over thirty million Moslems in Russia. Russia has declared itself an atheist nation. Christopher Columbus in this early voyage would set a holocaust for hemispheres in motion.

Expulsion of the Africans and Arabs from Spain would also set into motion the Inquisition. One of the slickest games in history was when certain Spaniards would tell certain people, especially the Grandees (the money managers of Spain, mostly Sephardic Jews), "Give me your money, or go to the gallows." Many Jews converted toCatholicism. They practiced Catholicism by day and Judaism by night. They were called the *marranos* or the "silent Jews."

Some of their descendants still live and are practicing both religions. The best known of their descendants is Fidel Castro. There's a good book on it published in France—there hasn't been an English translation—about Fidel Castro and his family, tracing his family back to the marranos. He will go through the motions of being Catholic, even now playing that wise game.

This expulsion will do Spain more harm than good because the Grandees—who were brought into Spain by the Africans and the Arabs—were doing a pretty good job of managing Spain's money. Spain has never had a strong economic system since they expelled the Grandees; they killed the goose that laid the golden egg. I can say across the board (maybe with the exception of Cuba): show me a Spanish-speaking country and I will show you a sloppily economically-run country...any place in the world.

Does anybody know a well-run country? They never got themselves together.

Another event would happen within Inner West Africa, the Western Sudan. The Emperor of the Songhai Empire, Sonni Ali, would be killed coming home from a minor war in the South. He drowned when his horse became entangled in underbrush, crossing a minor stream. Now the great independent states in Africa are beginning to fall. These states are not coastal states; these are Inner West African states. These states could have rescued West African states and saved them from the slave trade. They would go on to the heights of grandeur in the midst of the slave trade and in spite of the slave trade.

Christopher Columbus in 1492 set out for a new world. Let's ask some questions. This man has had no command position; he has not even been a petty officer. How then did this obscure sailor become Admiral of the Ocean Seas for the Spanish Navy? Who is behind this? Why is it that Christopher Columbus sailed from Spain the same week the Spanish expelled the Jews? Who exactly was Christopher Columbus? Was he sailing out ahead of the Expulsion?

Michael Bradley and others have now located those who financed the ships. They were all Jewish bankers who were told, "Give me your money, or give me your life." They were the chief translators on the boat. He was to go to Asia. Why didn't he go to Asia? Sailing up and down the Guinea Coast (West Africa), he had discovered—from African sailors who had already gone to the New World—there was a possibility of gold in another direction. I suspect that Columbus turned his ships in another direction. He also "discovered" that there was a current in the sea. If you pick it up at a certain time of year, it will push you almost straight into the Caribbean Islands. That current took him there. This is why ships were lost coming back, because if you come back too soon the current reverses itself once every six months. That's why he ended up in Portugal on his way back.

Once he got there—and you should read Eric Williams' *Documents of West Indian History*. This is the most underrated Caribbean scholar. Most people underrate him maybe because they didn't like the way he ran Trinidad and Tobago. I don't know how he ran Trinidad. I know he was a damn good researcher, one of the finest of the Caribbean researchers. I knew him at Howard, as a professor of Political Science. He was a brilliant man and he had a big ego. He was a very brilliant scholar, ego notwithstanding. *Documents of West Indian History* was only one of the four volumes he had compiled. He goes through Christopher Columbus' diary, the best analysis of Christopher Columbus' diary that I've ever seen. When Columbus saw these Indigenous Americans (mistakenly called Indians), he said in his monologue, "I wonder why they're bringing such small amounts of gold? I wonder where the mines are? They'll be easier to conquer than I thought they would be."

He would write a letter to Queen Isabella saying, "From this area I can send you as many slaves as you can accommodate." He never thought of partnership; in his mind it was enslavement from the very beginning. His intentions were not good. He would kill off his own labor supply. He would kill some of the people who could have helped him find the gold. For the documentation on this, I wish someone would read Father Bartolomeo de las Casas' work, the *Devastation of the Indies*. It's a small book and you could read it in one evening or less.

Father de las Casas is called the first historian of the New World. He wrote it all down. Christopher Columbus would go to him after the third voyage and the rapid disappearance of the Indians. He would go and ask for an increase in the African slave trade allegedly to save the soul of the Indians. When the pope would send Commissions to various islands sometimes not one Indian would be alive, but the African endured. If the African endured and the Indian perished it had nothing to do with the fact that one was braver than the other. It had to do with the structure of their societies.

The Indians had a monolithic society and the African came out of a pluralistic society, many societies functioning side by side. The Indian came out of a monolithic society which was tightly woven. While they existed side by side with the other societies, they did not give the other societies the same integration or recognition. Sometimes they waged relentless war against the neighboring society.

However, now the aborigine is rapidly disappearing. Father de las Casas said that from twelve to twenty-five million people were killed. We're just talking about the Caribbean Islands alone. We're not talking about South America, although he alludes to Mexico and South America; but his main concentration is on the Caribbean Islands.

Christopher Columbus would go from one place to the other. He "thought" Cuba was Japan. He was sent to the East Indies and would end up in the "West Indies." He told his sailors to sign a document that they were in the East Indies and if they didn't sign, he would cut their tongue out. Ivan Van Sertima has done an informative and concise chapter on this in his book, *They Came Before Columbus.* When we look at this man and what he has set in motion, he set in motion the increase in the African slave trade. The British had not entered the slave trade at first because the British had some difficulty with the Catholic Church. However, once the British decided to establish a church of their own and if you're of British extraction and belong to the Church of England you have to live with the fact that here's a church whose foundation was the hot sexual passions of Henry VIII. If anybody wants to prove otherwise, I'll hear them.

Henry VIII wanted to cut off one wife's head and wanted to marry another one. He wanted all these wives; he wanted justification. He wanted a church that would back him up in all his skullduggery, including his thievery, his raid on the Church treasury. So he created the kind of church that would give him what he wanted: the Church of England. Throughout his career he defended the Church as so sacred; it was sacred to him because it let him do what he wanted to do. He referred to the Church as though it were synonymous with the State. The Queen whose head he cut off was the only one that gave him a child that survived. That child was Elizabeth I. Someone called her the (alleged) Virgin Queen of England. We won't discuss that any further. They showed her a ledger of what could be made in the slave trade after she had refused to go into the business and finally she went into the business. One of the ships was her personal property, the good ship "Jesus" commanded by Captain John Hawkins. Britain came into the slave trade and made it a business, a dirty business, but a business. They are well organized gangsters with territory.

The British sailed up the Gambia River and took ten miles on each side. That's the little facsimile nation that is called The Gambia, right now; it was never a viable nation in the true sense. They would spread their slaveholding further west. They would push the Portuguese out of the West African slave trade.

What about the world Christopher Columbus set in motion? He set in motion western racism. He set in motion the colonization not only of history, but also the information about history. All of the fight over curricula was set in motion because Christopher Columbus and others set in motion a concept of divine White right/manifest destiny. The assumption that the people of Europe had rights over other people. It set in motion another bogus concept of a "chosen" people by God.

If God chooses one people over another people, then God is a bigot. You cannot say this is also a God of love. God is kind, God is no respecter of kith and kin and say, "God chose me to do something." Then while people are choosing, inasmuch as all "chosen" people "chose" themselves, why in the hell don't you choose yourself to be free?

Why won't you make a choice and say, "We are too proud to live in slums." Why don't you understand what went wrong with the world Christopher Columbus did not discover? Why can't we understand how other people rose from the bottom and recovered what belonged to them?

1 The Nature of the Gathering Storm

IN THIS YEAR OF THE QUINCENTENARY OF Christopher Columbus' alleged "discovery" of the Caribbean Islands and the Americas, collectively called the New World, there is a need not only to re-examine the myth of Columbus but the broader myth of Europe and its people and the consequences of their expansion beyond their shores in the 15th and the 16th century. This event needs an explanation over and above the fact of their expansion.

As a classroom teacher, I have referred to the years between 1400 and 1600 as the Christopher Columbus Era. I know full well that this era started before Columbus was born. This was a point in history when Europeans freed themselves from the lethargy of the Middle Ages, the aftermath of the Crusades and the famines and plagues that had taken one-third of the population of Europe. It is also the period when Europeans freed themselves from almost a thousand-year fear of Islam and what they referred to as the Infidel Arabs who had been controlling the Mediterranean and its trade routes since the decline of the Roman Empire in the middle of the 7th century. The renewal of European nationalism, the marriage of Ferdinand and Isabella of Spain, the expulsion of the Arabs, Moors and the Jews from Spain in 1492 and the introduction of the slave trade gave Europe a new economic lease on life. Europeans had to create a rationale and a series of myths to justify their new position and what they intended to extract from non-European people.

Some of the myths set in motion by what I have referred to as the Columbus Era still plague the world today. With the Atlantic Slave Trade the Europeans had set in motion a holocaust for African people that is still active in some form on the 500th year anniversary of Christopher Columbus' alleged "discovery." They had also set in motion an era of protracted genocide against non-European people that continues, with its many dimensions, in every place in the world where there is European influence over non-European people.

At this point there is a need to call attention to Michael Bradley's work, *The Iceman Inheritance,* that deals very frankly with the rise and expansion of European racism and the book by Frances Cress Welsing, *The Isis Papers,* that deals more specifically with the origins of White racism and how it affects African people.

There weren't enough soldiers in Europe to take over the continent of Africa, India, the Caribbean Islands and both South and North America. The greatest achievement of the Europeans was the conquest of the *mind* of their victims through a series of myths that could bear re-examining in order to understand the deeper meaning of the Christopher Columbus Era and its reverberations for today.

1. *The myth of a people waiting in darkness for another people to bring them the light.* In most countries where the Europeans invaded or influenced they put out the light of local civilizations and culture and destroyed civilizations, civilizations that were old before Europeans were born.

2. *The myth of a people without a legitimate God.* Europeans made no serious attempt to understand the religious cultures of non-European people wherever they went in the world. If their god concept was not in agreement with the Europeans, then the Europeans assured them that they had no god worthy of worship.

3. *The myth of the primitive and the aborigine.* Here we have a misinterpretation of two words that originally meant

"first" or the original. European interpretation was derogatory and downgrading, and it still is. In many ways the Europeans were saying to non-European people that they did not have the right to choose a god or a culture different from that of the Europeans.

4. *The myth of the invader and conqueror as civilizer.* Generally speaking, no people ever spread any civilization anywhere or at anytime in human history through invasion and conquest. The invader and the conqueror spreads his way of life at the expense of his victims. They generally destroy civilization in the name of civilization.

In this initial expansion, the Europeans not only colonized history, they colonized information about history. The most disastrous of all their colonizations was the colonization of the image of God. They denied the conquered people the right to see God through their own imagination or to address God in a word that came from their own language. Every effort was made to wipe from their memory how they ruled a state and how they related to their spirituality before the coming of the Europeans. Most of the people of the world were forced to forget that over half of human history was over before anyone knew that a European was in the world. Non-Europeans, especially in Nile Valley civilizations, had laid the basis for the spirituality that would later be converted into the major religions of the world. They had also developed the thought pattern that would later be developed into the philosophical thought of the world. All of this had happened outside of Europe before Europeans had names, durable shoes or houses with windows.

In order to understand Christopher Columbus, the African Holocaust and the protracted era of genocide set in motion by the Christopher Columbus Era, we must re-examine the year 1492 and give it a significance over and above what happened in Europe.

At this point, it is essential that we look back in order to look forward with more understanding. Too many times it is assumed that African history began with the slave trade. There were a thousand years of independent state formation and state management in Inner West Africa called the Western Sudan before the slave trade. This period of independent African political and cultural activity needs to be reviewed in order to understand, at least in part, what West Africa lost in the slave trade. Professor Van Sertima has said that African history has been locked into a 500-year room. I have extended this by saying that African history has been locked behind a slavery curtain. It is necessary to look at West African history before and after the slave trade in order to understand how and why the slave trade occurred and why African people, more than any other people in the world, were its main victims. The Africans were open-minded and politically naive in their relationship with non-African people, especially the European. So they did not know the intentions and the temperament of the Europeans then and they do not know it now.

2 Africa Before the Slave Trade

MY APPROACH TO THIS SUBJECT, on reflection, might seem overly ambitious because most of the writers who have dealt with the African slave trade that began in the fifteenth and sixteenth centuries have not acknowledged that an age of grandeur came before this agony that changed Africa and the world for all time to come.

When I speak of Africa's age of grandeur I am referring to the last flowering of state and empire-building in the Western Sudan (Inner West Africa) before the breaking-up of the coastal states and the spread of the slave trade to other areas. This is the forgotten age of grandeur whose loss helped to make the West African slave trade possible.

I generally divide African history into three arbitrary categories. There is nothing scientific about my method. It is a utility developed in order to simplify an overall approach to African history. In dividing African history into ages of grandeur that I call the First, Second and Third Golden Age, I am saying to students that most people in the world who have had an age of grandeur or a Golden Age, have had only one. As did the Romans, the Greeks rose and fell and never rose again. I maintain that African people have had three Golden Ages and could have a fourth one. What does this say about our potential and our ability to bounce back from defeat and decline and be a total people again?

There is a need now to look back on Africa's Golden Ages and the main currents of African history that led to the decline of the last age of grandeur and the beginning of the slave trade.

It can be said with a strong degree of certainty that Africa has had three Golden Ages. The first two reached their climax and were in decline before Europe as a functioning entity in human society was born. Africa's First Golden Age began at "the beginning" with the birth of man and the development of organized societies. It is generally conceded in most scholarly circles that mankind originated in Africa; this provides a basis for the theory that African man was the father and African woman the mother of humankind.

In his book, *The Progress and Evolution of Man in Africa*, Dr. L. S. B. Leakey states that:

> "In every country that one visits and where one is drawn into a conversation about Africa, the question is regularly asked by people who should know better: `But what has Africa contributed to world progress?' The critics of Africa forget that men of science today, with few exceptions, are satisfied that Africa was the birthplace of man himself, and that for many hundreds of centuries thereafter, Africa was in the forefront of all human progress." (Leakey, 1961:1)

In the early development of man, the family was the most important unit in existence. Through the years the importance of this unit has not changed. The first human societies were developed for reasons relating to the needs and survival of the family. The early African had to make hooks to catch fish, spears to hunt with, and knives. He searched for new ways of building shelter, gathering and raising food, and domesticating animals. Our use of fire today simply continues the process started by the early Africans—the control of fire. In the making of tools that sets man apart from all living creatures Africans started man along the tool-making path.

With the discovery of metals and how to use them, all Africa took a great leap forward. Man had learned how to take iron from the ground and turn it into spears and tools. Iron cultures spread rapidly across Africa and there were very few parts of Africa that were not influenced by these iron age cultures. Iron cultures had their greatest development in the area of Africa that is now the Eastern Sudan in the great city-state of Meroe. The use of iron accelerated every aspect of African development and introduced a new danger—the eventual use of iron weapons in warfare. (Phillipson, 1977 102-227)

The Nile River became a great cultural highway, bringing peoples and cultures out of inner Africa. These migrations by river led to the establishment of one of the greatest nations in world history—Egypt. In his book, *The Destruction of Black Civilization, Great Issues of a Race from 4500 B.C. to 2000 A.D.*, the African-American historian, Chancellor Williams (1974), refers to Egypt as "Ethiopia's oldest daughter," and calls attention to the evidence to prove the southern African origin of early Egyptian people and their civilization. (62-124)

Egypt first became an organized nation about 6000 B.C. Medical interest centers upon a period in the Third Dynasty (5345-5307 B.C.), when Egypt had an ambitious pharaoh named Zoser; and Zoser, in turn, had for his chief counsel and minister a brilliant commoner named Imhotep (whose name means "He who cometh in peace"). Although Egypt gave the world some of the greatest personalities in the history of mankind, Imhotep is singularly outstanding. In the ancient history of Egypt, no individual left a deeper impression than the commoner Imhotep. He was the world's first multi-genius. He was also the real father of medicine. Imhotep constructed the famous step pyramid of Sakkarah near Memphis and the building methods used in the construction of this pyramid revolutionized the architecture of the ancient world (Jackson, 1978: 3-35). In his book, *Evolution of Modern Medicine*, Sir William Osler (1921) refers to Imhotep as "the first figure of a physician to stand out clearly from the mists of antiquity."

The period in Egyptian history from the Third Dynasty to the first invasion of Egypt by the Hyksos, or Shepherd Kings, in 1675 B.C. is, in my opinion, the apex of the First Golden Age. The Western Asian domination over Egypt lasted about four hundred and twenty years and was ended by the rise of Egyptian nationalism during the Seventeenth Dynastian era. It would later develop into a state with a known history of more than a thousand years.

In Europe and in the Arab countries, Ghana was known as a country rich in gold. This was a natural attraction for the Arabs and later the Europeans. The country reached the height of its greatness during the reign of Tenkamenin one of its greatest kings, who came to power in 1062 A.D. The king lived in a palace of stone and wood which was built to be defended in time of war. The Empire was well organized. The political progress and social well-being of its people could be favorably compared to the best kingdoms and empires that prevailed in Europe at this time. The country had a military force of 200,000 men. (Wingfield, 1957)

In one of a number of holy wars, or jihads, Ghana was invaded by the Almoravides under the leadership of Abu Bekr of the Sosso Empire in 1076, A.D. This conquest brought an end to Ghana's age of prosperity and cultural development. The character of the country was slow to change. Nearly a hundred years later the Arab writer, El Idrisi, wrote of it as being "the greatest kingdom of the Blacks" (Buah, 1974: 171). In a later account, El Idrisi said: "Ghana is the most commercial of the Black countries. It is visited by rich merchants from all the surrounding countries and from the extremities of the West" (Buah, 1974: 6).

In 1087 Ghana regained its independence, but without regaining its old strength, state organization, and grandeur. The ruins of the Empire of Ghana became the kingdoms of Diara and Sosso. The provinces of Ghana became a part of the Mali Empire and were later absorbed into the Songhai Empire.

The great drama of state building, trade and commerce and power brokerage unfolded at Timbuktoo, the queen city of the Western Sudan. Two hundred miles down the Niger from Timbuktu the competing city of Gao stood. It was founded about the 7th century A.D. and was the capital of the large Black empire of Songhai. Like Timbuktu, it was in a favorable position for the trans-Saharan trade in the days of the regular caravans from North Africa. Also, like Timbuktu, the greatest days of Gao came in the fifteenth and sixteenth centuries. (DuBois, 1969: 189-274)

In the years when Timbuktoo was the great intellectual nucleus of the Songhai Empire, African scholars were enjoying a renaissance that was known and respected throughout most of

Africa and in parts of Europe. At this period in African history, the University of Sankore was the educational capital of the Western Sudan. In his book, *Timbuktoo the Mysterious,* Felix DuBois gives us the following picture:

> "The scholars of Timbuktoo yielded in nothing to the saints and their sojourns in the foreign universities of Fez, Tunis and Cairo. They astounded the most learned men in Islam by their erudition. That these Negroes were on a level with the Arabian savants is proved by the fact that they were installed as professors in Morocco and Egypt. In contrast to this, we find that the Arabs were not always equal to the requirements of Sankore." (DuBois, 1969: 275)

The famous Emperor of Mali, Mansa Mussa stopped at Timbuktu on his pilgrimage to Mecca in 1324. He went in regal splendor with an entourage of 60,000 persons, including 1200 servants. Five hundred bondsman, each of whom carried a staff of pure gold, marched in front of the Emperor. Two hundred eighty camels bore 2,400 pounds of gold which this African monarch distributed as alms and gifts. Mussa returned from Mecca with an architect who designed imposing buildings in Timbuktu and other parts of his realm. (Boahen, 1969: 9-17)

To the outside world of the late medieval period, the Emperor Mansa Mussa was more than an individual. He was Africa. He conquered the Songhai Empire and rebuilt the University of Sankore. He figured, by name, on every map. In his lifetime he became the symbol of the mystery and the fabulous wealth of the unknown African continent. He was the most colorful of the Black kings of the fourteenth century. He still held this position nearly two centuries after his death.

After the death of Mansa Mussa the Empire of Mali declined in importance. Its place was taken by Songhai whose greatest king was Askia the Great (Mohammed Toure). Askia came to power in 1493, one year after Columbus landed in America. He consolidated the territory conquered by the previous ruler Sonni Ali and built Songhai into the most powerful state in the Western Sudan. His realm, it is said, was larger than all Europe.

The German writer, Henry Barth, in his famous work, *Travels and Discoveries in North and Central Africa* (1857) calls Askia the

Great "one of the most brilliant and enlightened administrators of all times" (667). He reorganized the army of Songhai, improved the system of banking and credit, and made the city-states of Gao Walata, Timbuktu and Jenne into intellectual centers. Timbuktu, during his reign, was a city of more than 100,000 people, a city "filled to the top," says a chronicler of that time, "with gold and dazzling women." (Felix Dubois: 250)

Askia encouraged scholarship and literature. Students from all over the Moslem world came to Timbuktoo to study grammar, law and surgery at the University of Sankore; scholars came from North Africa and Europe to confer with learned historians and writers of this Black empire. Many books were written and a Sudanese literature developed. Leo Africanus, who wrote one of the best known works on the Western Sudan says:

> "In Timbuktoo there are numerous judges, doctors and clerics, all receiving good salaries from the king. He pays great respect to men of learning. There is a big demand for books in manuscript, imported from Barbary [North Africa]. More profit is made from the book trade than from any other line of business."

Askia has been hailed as one of the wisest monarchs of the Middle Ages. Alexander Chamberlain (1911), in his book, *The Contribution of the Negro to Human Civilization*, says of him:

> "In personal character, in administrative ability, in devotion to the welfare of his subjects, in open-mindedness towards foreign influences, and in wisdom in the adoption of enlightened ideas and institutions from abroad, King Askia was certainly the equal of the average European monarch of the time and superior to many of them." (489)

After the death of Askia the Great in 1528, the Songhai Empire began to lose its strength and its control over its vast territory. When the Songhai Empire collapsed after the capture of Timbuktu and Gao by the Moroccans in 1591, the whole of the Western Sudan was devastated by the invading troops. The Sultan of Morocco, El-Mansur had sent a large army with

European firearms across the Sahara to attack the once powerful empire of Songhai. The army did not reach Timbuktu until 1591. The prosperous city of Timbuktu was plundered by the army of freebooters. A state of anarchy prevailed. The University of Sankore, which had stood for over five hundred years, was destroyed and the faculty exiled to Morocco. The greatest Sudanese scholar of that day, Ahmed Baba was among those exiled. Baba was a scholar of great depth and inspiration. He was the author of more than forty books on such diverse themes as theology, astronomy, ethnography and biography. His rich library of 1600 books was lost during his expatriation from Timbuktu. (Clarke, 1977: 142-147)

Timbuktu provides the most tragic example of the struggles of the West African states and towns as they strove to preserve what was once their Golden Age. The Arabs, Berbers and Tuaregs from the north showed them no mercy. Timbuktu had previously been sacked by the Tuaregs as early as 1433 and they had occupied it for thirty years. Between 1591 and 1593, the Tuaregs once more occupied and looted Timbuktu. Thus, Timbuktu, once the queen city of the Western Sudan with more than two hundred thousand inhabitants and the center of a powerful state, degenerated into a shadow of its former stature.

Now, West Africa entered a sad period of decline. During the Moorish occupation, wreck and ruin became the order of the day. When the Europeans arrived in this part of Africa and saw these conditions they assumed that nothing of order and value had existed in these countries. The past Golden Ages are part of the history that the exploiters of Africa want the world to ignore. The great Ghanaian scholar, Dr. Joseph B. Danquah, outlined the pre-slavery history of Africa in his introduction to the book, *United West Africa (or Africa) at the Bar of the Family of Nations,* when he said:

"By the time Alexander the Great was sweeping the civilized world with conquest after conquest from Chaeronia to Gaza from Babylon to Cabul; by the time this first of the Aryan conquerors was learning the rudiments of war and government at the feet of philosophic Aristotle; and by the time Athens was laying down the foundations of modern European civilization, the earliest and greatest Ethiopian culture had already flourished and dominated the civilized world for over four centuries and a half. Imperial Ethiopia had conquered Egypt and founded the XXVth Dynasty, and for a century and a half the central seat of civilization in the known world was held by the ancestors of the modern Negro, maintaining and defending it against the Assyrian and Persian Empires of the East. Thus, at the time when Ethiopia was leading the civilized world in culture and conquest, East was East, but West was not, and the first European (Graecian) Olympiad was as yet to be held. Rome was nowhere to be seen on the map, and sixteen centuries were to pass before Charlemagne would rule in Europe and Egbert become first King of England. Even then, history was to drag on for another seven hundred weary years, before Roman Catholic Europe could see fit to end the Great Schism soon to be followed by the disturbing news of the discovery of America and by the fateful rebirth of the youngest of World Civilizations."

In this young civilization, a need for slavery was created. This need had an unforeseen effect upon African people, the magnitude of which continues to be experienced to the present day.

When the Europeans first came down the west coast of Africa they were treated as guests by the unsuspecting Africans whom they would later enslave. When the Africans began to suspect that the intentions of the Europeans were not good, in most cases, it was too late and they did not have the modern weapons of that day to defend themselves.

In his book, *Ghana, The Morning After*, K. Budu-Acquah (1960) explains the effort of one king of the country that would later be called The Gold Coast (now Ghana) to save his people from the slave trade. His name was Nana Kwamena Ansa. His attempt to discourage the Portuguese from settling in his country was met with force. The following is Budu-Acquah's explanation of his effort:

"Our forefathers' antipathy to Imperialism is exemplified by the speech of Nana Ansa, who foresaw clearly that they were going to be called upon to prey on one another, to be left helpless, disorganized and demoralized. His speech has been quoted by the late Mr. Mensah-Sarbah Dr. de Graft Johnson and others, and it is worth quoting once more from W.W. Claridge's *History of the Gold Coast and Ashanti* for it shows equally well the development of the Akan language, its poetry which is `as perfect and musical as any Latin or Roman language' and `if the richness of a language be an index to the natural eloquence of the Akan people it is a sure indication of a balanced and highly developed mental equipment."

In his speech to Diego de Azambuia, commander of the Portuguese expedition, King Ansa said:

"I am not insensible to the high honour which your great master the Chief of Portugal has this day conferred upon me. His friendship I have always endeavored to merit by the strictness of my dealings with the Portuguese and by my constant exertions to procure an immediate lading for the vessels. But never until this day did I observe such a difference in the appearance of his subjects; they have hitherto been meanly attired; were easily contented with the commodity they received; and so far from wishing to continue in this country, were never happy until they could complete their lading and return. Now I remark a strange difference. A great number, richly dressed, are anxious to be allowed to build houses, and to continue among us. Men of such eminence, conducted by a commander who from his own account seems to have descended from the God who made day and night, can never bring themselves to endure the hardships of this climate nor would they here be able to procure any of the luxuries that abound in their own country. The passions that are common to us all men will therefore inevitably bring on disputes and it is far preferable that both our nations should continue on the same footing as they hitherto have done, allowing your ships to come and go as usual; the desire of seeing each other occasionally will preserve peace between us. The sea and the land being always neighbors are continually at variance and contending who shall give way; the sea with great violence attempting to subdue the land, and the land with equal obstinacy resolving to oppose the sea." (Budu-Acquah, 1960: 23-24)

The Portuguese were not impressed by the eloquence of King Ansa's speech. They forced their way into his country and built the first permanent slave trading settlement in West Africa. The year was 1482.

K. Budu-Acquah explains the tragedy in the following statement:

"This was the beginning of European colonization, the beginning of the hunting-ground for procuring slave labor, the disruption of our religion, our social systems, the lost of respect for our forefathers; all these things being taken away without anything of value being put in their place." (1960: 24)

It is evident then that European colonization was instrumental in bringing about the decline of the Third of Africa's Golden Ages. Therefore, this history of exploitation and the responsibility for the present condition of the societies of the Third Golden Age are understandably attributed to the greed and imperialistic goals of the European nations.

3 New Enemies Disguised As Friends

THE GHANIAN WRITER, A. Adu Boahen, in the article, "*The Coming of the Europeans*" *(c. 1440-1700)* gives us the following information about this significant event in history:

"Africa south of the Sahara has been known to Europeans since Greco-Roman times, but it was not until the fourth decade of the fifteenth century that they began to arrive in numbers on its shores. The first to come were the Portuguese. They were followed in the 1450's by the Spaniards, who soon after abandoned Africa to explore the Americas, toward the end of the century some English and French adventurers and traders arrived. However, their governments were not to give official backing to such enterprises until the sixteenth and seventeenth centuries. The Dutch were the next to appear on the African scene, and during the last decade of the sixteenth century they effectively challenged the lead enjoyed by the Portuguese. The Danes dropped anchor in 1642, the Swedes in 1647, and the Brandenburgers in 1682. The reasons for this sudden surge of interest were partly political, partly economic, partly technological. In the first place, no overseas activities could succeed without the patronage and direction of a strong nation-state enjoying stable and peaceful conditions at home, and no such nation-states emerged in Europe until after the end of the fourteenth century and these continued to be wracked by foreign and civil wars for another hundred years or more."

The nation-states of Europe stabilized themselves and developed their economy mainly at the expense of African people. Professor Boahen further tells us that:

"On balance then, politically, economically, and socially, the European presence and activities in Africa during the second period were virtually an unmitigated disaster for the Africans. By 1700 all the great hopes that had been conjured up during the earlier phase of exploration had turned sour. To borrow Basil Davidson's terms, Africa had by then turned into the "Black Mother," producing slaves solely in the interest of the growing capitalist system in Europe and the New World and it was to do this for another hundred and fifty years. At the beginning of their contact, sub-Saharan Africa was politically, culturally, and artistically comparable to Europe. By 1700 Europe had leaped forward technologically and socially, but Africa and its Black peoples had become paralyzed and impoverished, a tragedy from which they still have not recovered."

In his pamphlet, *The Man Who Stole A Continent,* John Weatherwax spoke collectively of the British entry into the slave trade. While he used a single figure in relationship to this entry, he was actually referring to the collective assault of Europeans on the west coast of Africa and how the slave trade became a three-continent industry:

"There was a man who stole a continent. Being cruel as well as greedy, and possessing power, *he enslaved twenty million of its people,* sending them over the ocean—ten million to the Eastern Hemisphere and ten million to the Western Hemisphere.

In the process of capturing the twenty million people whom he sold, *eighty million other people died*—some during slave raids (for when a village was raided, often the very young and very old and the sick were killed), some from exposure, disease and grief during shipment abroad, and some by suicide at the water's edge or in transit.

The sale of *twenty million human beings* as slaves gave the man hundreds of millions of treasure. But this was only the start of his enrichment.

48

He and his children and grandchildren and those to whom they sold slaves received much, much more (many billions more) through the *unpaid labor* of whole generations of slaves. But this, too, was not at all the end of their enrichment."

Professor Weatherwax concludes his analysis of the start of the slave trade in the following manner:

"For the morality of *The Man Who Stole a Continent* and of his children and grandchildren and agents can only be characterized as the *Most Way-Out Evil this world has ever known.* And Way-Out Evil is Satanic, and has only one possible end: to be cast out altogether and forever from the society known as humankind; to be cast into the burning fire which is its natural home to be remembered only (by the generations which follow its end) *as the most devastating catastrophe that ever befell mankind.*"

The events described by John Weatherwax were the beginning of the African Holocaust and a period of protracted genocide that would change the political character of the world for all times to come.

4 Slave Trade and Slavery In Retrospect

IN THIS SHORT APPRAISAL OF CHRISTOPHER COLUMBUS and the African Holocaust, I have reopened and re-examined a much written about subject that is still misunderstood by most people. The basis of this misunderstanding is in the fact that most students of this subject look upon the African slave trade as though it were the only system of slavery known to man. Slavery is an old institution and there are no people who have not at some time in history been a victim of it.

The African slave trade can best be understood if we at least take a brief look at the historical roots of slavery as a world institution.

Slavery in ancient societies was appreciably different from the type of slavery that was introduced into Africa by the Europeans in the fifteenth and sixteenth centuries. In most ancient societies the slave was held in servitude for a limited time, for specific reasons, and, in most cases, the slaves were captured in local wars. Skin color was not a factor as to whether a person did or did not become a slave and, in most cases, the slave had some rights that the master had to respect. In ancient Egypt, Kush, Greece, and early Rome there were clearly defined codes of conduct governing the relationship between the slaves and their masters. Some of the earliest of these codes are recorded in the laws of Moses.

In the book *The History of Slavery and the Slave Trade* by W. O. Blake, published in 1858, the following information relating to early slavery is revealed:

> "The Mosaic institutions were rather predicated upon the previous existence of slavery in the surrounding nations, than designed to establish it for the first time and the provisions of the Jewish law upon this subject, effected changes and modifications which must have improved the condition of slaves among that particular people. There were various modes by which the Hebrews might be reduced to servitude. A poor man might sell himself; a father might sell his children; debtors might be delivered as slaves to their creditors; thieves who were unable to make restitution for the property stolen were sold for the benefit of the sufferers. Prisoners of war were subjected to servitude and if a Hebrew captive was redeemed by another Hebrew from a Gentile, he might be sold to another Israelite. At the return of the year of jubilee, all Jewish captives were set free. However, by some writers it is stated that this did not apply to foreign slaves held in bondage as, over those the master had entire control. The law of Moses provides that 'if a man smite his servant or his maid with a rod, and he die under his hand he shall be surely punished.' This restriction is said, by some, to have applied only to Hebrew slaves, and not to foreign captives who were owned by Jews. Mosaic laws declared the terms upon which a Hebrew, who had been sold, could redeem himself or be redeemed by his friends and his right to take with him his wife and children, when discharged from bondage."

The main point of this reference is that the slaves of the ancient world were considered with some humanity. This was nonetheless true of ancient Asia and Africa. In fact, in Africa, in both ancient and modern times, slaves have been known to rise above their servitude and become kings in the very houses in which they had been slaves.

The fact that slavery existed in West Africa prior to contact with Europeans is often used to excuse the European slave trade. The two systems had few similarities. The tragic and distinguishing feature of the slave trade that was introduced by the European was that it totally dehumanized the slave. This dehumanization continued in many ways throughout the slavery period and well into the colonial era. This crucial act was supported by a rationale that was created in part by the Christian church and later extended by the writers of the seventeenth and eighteenth century. The myth of a people with no history and culture comes out of this period. All myths are contagious and one can create many others. This fact can be better understood after some insight into how and why the slave trade came to be.

Early in the fifteenth century, Europe began to recover from the wounds of the Middle Ages and the Crusades. European skill in ship-building had improved and, in search of a food supply for their hungry population and for new worlds to conquer, Europeans began to venture beyond their shores. There are many reasons why the Europeans had not embarked upon worldwide exploration before this time: their ships were small and unsafe for long sea journeys; oars were sometimes used to propel these ships and the outcome of all voyages depended largely on the wind; there were no good maps or instruments to guide sailors through unknown waters.

At that time most Europeans were ignorant about the shape of the world and some of them thought it was flat. The Portuguese set out to disprove this and, about the middle of the fifteenth century, they began trading with the people along the west coast of Africa, to which they gave the name "guinea" after the Sudanic Empire of Ghana. At first they traded mainly in gold, but before long they began to take slaves also.

Social and political unrest began to develop among some of the nations of West Africa at the time Europe was regaining its strength and a degree of unity. The first Europeans to visit the west coast of Africa did not have to fight their way in—they came as guests and were treated as guests. Later they decided to stay as conquerors and slave traders. In order to gain a position strong enough to attain these ambitions, they began to take sides in African family disputes, very often supplying the family or tribe they favored with arms and using their favorites as slave catchers. A number of African nations went into the slave trade in order to buy guns and other European manufactured items. Others were forced to capture slaves or become slaves.

The Europeans did not come to Africa initially to find slaves. For years they had been hearing stories about the great riches of Africa. At the Battle of Cueta against the Moslems in 1415, Prince Henry of Portugal, who later became known as Prince Henry the Navigator, heard about the prosperity of Timbuktu and the wealth of the great states along the west coast of Africa. He also heard stories about a great African Christian king named Prester John.

Before the end of the fifteenth century, the Portuguese sailors had come to know the general shape of the continent of Africa. They traded regularly with African countries from 1471 on. Forts were built along the coast of West Africa. The most famous of these forts, still in existence, is Elmina Castle in what is now Ghana. This fort was started in 1482 by a Portuguese captain, Don Diego de Azambuia. Because of the large profits gained by the Portuguese in their trading in this country, they called it the Gold Coast.

During the latter half of the fifteenth century, European nationalism was reflected in the expansion of trade in both sales and manufactured goods. The marriage of Queen Isabella and King Ferdinand gave Europe the unity to drive out the Arabs and the Moors. Both Spain and Portugal were becoming powerful Mediterranean nations.

In 1488, Bartholomew Diaz had sailed around the southern tip of Africa. About ten years later, another Portuguese sailor, Vasco da Gama, sailed past the point reached by Diaz. With the help of an Arab pilot, Vasco da Gama reached India in 1498. For Europe, the door to the vast world of Asia was open.

The rationale for justifying the slave trade had already started in Europe with Europeans attempting to justify the enslavement of other Europeans. This is a neglected aspect of history that is rarely taken into consideration. There was a concerted effort to obtain European labor to open up the vast regions of the New World. In what became the United States, White enslavement started before Black enslavement. In an article, "White Servitude in the United States," published in *Ebony* in November 1969, the Afro-American historian, Lerone Bennett Jr., gives the following information about this period:

"When someone removes the cataracts of whiteness from our eyes, and when we look with unclouded vision on the bloody shadows of the American past, we will recognize for the first time that the Afro-American, who was so often second in freedom, was also second in slavery. Indeed, it will be revealed that the African-American was third in slavery. For he inherited his chains, in a manner of speaking, from the pioneer bondsmen, who were red and white."

The enslavement of both red men and White men in the early American colonies was a contradiction of English law. The colonies were founded with the understanding that neither chattel slavery nor villeinage would be recognized. Yet forced labor was widely used in England. This system was transferred to the colonies and used to justify a form of slavery that was visited upon red and White men. Concise information on this system and how it developed is revealed in the book, *Slavery and Abolition, 1831-1841*, by Albert Bushnell first published in 1906.

It was decreed that the apprentice must serve his seven years, and take floggings as his master saw fit; the hired servant must carry out his contract for his term of service. Convicts of the state, often including political offenders, were slaves of the state and were sometimes sold to private owners overseas. The colonists claimed those rights over some of their White fellow countrymen. There was a large class of "redemptioners" who had agreed that their service should be sold for a brief term of years to pay their passage-money, and of "indentured" or "indented" servants, brought by their masters under legal obligation, who served even longer terms, subject to the same penalties of branding, whipping, and mutilation as African slaves. These forms of servitude were supposed to be limited in duration and transmitted no claim to the servant's children. In spite of this servitude, the presumption, in law, was that a White man was born free.

The English settlers had, at once, begun to enslave their Indian neighbors, soothing their consciences with the argument that it was right to make slaves of pagans. In large numbers, the Indians fled or died in captivity, leaving few of their descendants in bondage. The virgin soil of the new English settlements continued to need more labor. This led to a fierce search for White labor that subsequently led to a search for Black labor.

Bennett continues: "It has been estimated that at least two out of every three White colonists worked for a term of years in the fields or kitchens as semi-slaves... White servitude was the historic foundation upon which the system of Black slavery was constructed."

There is a need to examine the slave trade and slavery and the role of Christopher Columbus and his voyages in setting this great tragedy in motion. I am attempting to examine the slave trade and slavery with fresh insight and with a focus on long neglected aspects of this subject. Africans played a major role in opening up the New World for European settlement. Their labor and the raw material taken from their countries were important features in the development of the European Industrial Revolution.

5 The Slave Trade: How and Why It Started

TO UNDERSTAND THE AFRICAN SLAVE TRADE we must understand slavery as an institution—an institution almost as old as human society. Every people, sometime or another, have been slaves. In fact, Europeans enslaved other Europeans for a much longer period than they enslaved Africans. Slavery was a permanent feature of the ancient world, in Egypt, Kush, and Rome.

The African slave period is best known to us because it is the best-documented. However, these documents are often confusing because they were created by people who were trying to justify the slave trade. Most people, especially Europeans who created most of the documents on slave trade, write about the subject with the intent to make the victim of slavery feel guilty and to vindicate the perpetrators of the slave trade.

There is probably more dishonesty related to the interpretation of this subject than any other subject known to man. The African slave trade, like African history, is often written about but rarely understood. This misunderstanding probably grows out of the fact that we nearly always start the study of the African slave trade in the wrong place. The germ, the motive, the rationale for the African slave trade started in the minds of the Europeans in the fifteenth and the sixteenth centuries. The slave trade could not have started at all had there been no market for it. The slave trade started when the Europeans began to expand out into the broader world; the market was created by Europeans for European reasons.

The story of the African slave trade is essentially the story of the consequences of the second rise of Europe. In the years between the passing of the Roman Empire in the eighth century and the partial unification of Europe through the framework of the Catholic Church in the fifteenth century, Europeans were engaged mainly in internal matters. With the opening of the New World and the expulsion of the Arabs and the Moors from Spain during the latter part of the fifteenth century, the Europeans started to expand beyond their homeland into the broader world. They were searching for new markets, new materials, new manpower, and new land to exploit. The African slave trade was created to accommodate this expansion.

The basis for the European Industrial Revolution had already been established. They had already created embryo technology, including the gun. In the years that followed, they also used other advantages, mainly a large fleet of ships and rabble soldiers and sailors with no sentimental attachment to non-European people, to take over most of the world. In so doing, they destroyed a large number of nations and civilizations that were older than any in Europe.

The main problem with the African, in dealing with the European during this early period, was the African's tragic naiveté. He had never dealt extensively with this kind of people. He came out of a society where nature was kind; nature furnished him enough food, enough land, enough of the basic things he needed to live a pretty good life. These old African societies were governed by honor and obligation. Land could neither be bought or sold; there were no fights over the ownership of land. The land belonged to everyone.

The European, coming from a society where nature was rather stingy and where he had to compete with his brother for his breakfast, his land, and his woman, had acquired a competitive nature that the African could not deal with. In order to justify the destruction of these African societies, a monster that still haunts our lives was created. This monster was racism. The slave trade and the colonial system that followed are the parents of this

58

catastrophe. The Europeans, mainly the Portuguese, who came to the west coast of Africa in the fifteenth century, were not at first looking for slaves. The search for gold and other treasures lured them to Africa. They did not have to fight their way into the continent they came as guests and were treated as guests. Then they grew strong, decided to be conquerors, and turned on their hosts.

Another myth we have to dispel is that the Europeans came to Africa to spread civilization. Actually, most of the great civilizations in Africa declined after the coming of the Europeans. For years the Europeans had been hearing rumors about African cities of gold and beautiful women.

There were also legends circulated in Europe about a great emperor in Ethiopia called Prester John. But when the Portuguese arrived in Africa, Prester John had been dead for three hundred years and they looked for him on one side of Africa, and he had been on the other. But no European came to Africa to tame any raw savage. When the Europeans first saw the cities of Africa, they reported that these cities were well designed and that the African was civilized to the marrow of his bones.

Fifty years later, when they wanted to justify the slave trade they started the myths about savage Africa, with no organized societies, no cities, even no knowledge of the wheel. The European did not enter Africa to bring civilization. In fact, no nation ever invaded another nation for any reason other than to exploit that nation for its own reasons. This is true even when Whites invade Whites. It's true when Browns invade Browns. And it's also true when Blacks invade Blacks. The intent of every invader, no matter what his color, is to establish his own way of life and, in nearly every case, the local culture suffers.

This happened when the Europeans invaded the west coast of Africa. We have their word that they did not meet an uncivilized people. We also have their word that they encountered not only well-organized societies but societies that had a great deal of order and beauty.

In 1434, a small fleet of Portuguese ships sailed down the coast of Africa and established some trading posts. By 1441, they were taking some of the tropical riches out of Africa and also a few slaves they bought who had been prisoners of war captured.

in some local skirmishes among Africans. By 1482, they had built the fortress of Elmina Castle, the beginning of Forts built by Europeans along the coast of West Africa to protect themselves from the Africans when the slave trade was established. In fact, the slave trade did not really get under way until the Europeans had these fortresses built. And while building the forts, with the help of Africans, they were telling the Africans that they had come to deal in honorable trade and the naive Africans believed this story. These fortresses actually served as holding stations for the slaves that they were shipping to the New World. Incidentally, the Scandinavians entered the slave trade after the Portuguese but they did not have any appreciable success, and they became middlemen in the slave trade.

Then, when the Arabs and Moors were expelled from Spain, they returned to Africa—after being the masters of the Mediterranean for 750 years. They had no sentimental attachment to Africa. They began to prey on the nations south of the Sahara, principally the old empire of Songhai. They first claimed the salt mines, for salt was then so precious that traders gave two parts of gold for one part of salt. They sent troops from what is now Morocco down into this area. The fight over the salt mines at Taghaza on the edge of the Sahara Desert became a great political and economic struggle.

But something else happened, too. Christopher Columbus had, by sheer accident, started to look for the East Indies and instead found what was later called the West Indies. A new world was opened to Europeans, and they promptly began their exploitation.

6 Time of Troubles

AFRICA'S TIME OF TRAGEDY AND DECLINE STARTED both in Europe and in Africa itself. For more than a thousand years Africans had been bringing into being empire after empire. But the opening of Europe's era of exploration, Africa's own internal strife, and the slave trade turned what had been Africa's Golden Age into a time of troubles.

The Crusades may be called the beginning of Europe's reawakening. A religious fervor, not unrelated to politics, had stirred Europeans out of their lethargy and their indifference to the larger world. The First Crusade, begun in 1095, was precipitated by the Seljuk Turks, whose persecution of Christians had placed even Constantinople in jeopardy. The Eastern heads of the Church appealed to Pope Urban II for help. At a great Church council in France the pope pointed out that if Constantinople fell to the Turks, Western Europe would soon be overrun. He made an eloquent plea to the kings and princes gathered, and to all Western European Christendom, to rally to the aid of the Christians in the East and to drive the "infidels" from the Holy Land.

This religious crisis gave Europe a semblance of unity; and although it can be said that the Crusades were military and religious failures, they did provide the opportunity to bring new information to Europe. The religious wars also had a profound effect on the political development of Europe. The Western monarchs were able to strengthen their authority and develop a strong central government while many members of their turbulent aristocracies were fighting in the Holy Land.

Contact with the East had a deep and lasting effect on the Crusaders, who belonged to a civilization where culture and learning had almost vanished during the Dark Ages. The princes in their castles and the peasants in their huts were equally ignorant and uneducated. When they arrived in the East, they soon realized how backward were the people of the West. They marveled at the beautiful cities, the thriving commerce, the busy industries, the art, and the learning. The impetus for exploration was fueled by what the Crusaders met along the way. Ships built to ferry the Crusaders to the Holy Land returned laden with the products of the East. The cargoes of spices, fruits, rich silks, satins, velvets, and other luxury goods had found a ready market. Thus the Crusades brought into being the first attempts to open fresh trade routes to the East. Early in the fifteenth century Europeans, search of new worlds to conquer and of a food supply to feed the continent's hungry population, began to venture across the seas.

NORTH AFRICA: By 1492, North Africa was confronted with the painful fact of its waning influence in Mediterranean Europe. Spain and Portugal, which had broken the yoke of North African domination, were asserting themselves as powerful, independent nations with colonial aspirations in the lands of their former conquerors. Islam, a great religious and military force in North Africa and the Middle East since the latter part of the seventh century, was torn apart by internal strife and bickering. The relationship of North Africa to the people of the Western Sudan was deteriorating. For hundreds of years this relationship had been good. Africans from the Western Sudan had participated in large numbers in the conquest of Spain in the year A.D. 711. These Africans made up the major military force that kept Spain under North African domination, and they participated in that country's intellectual life, as is still reflected in Spain's art, culture, and literature.

In order to understand this neglected aspect of history—the role of Africans in the conquering and ruling of Spain—it is necessary to go back in time to retell, at least briefly, the part that Black Africans played in the rise of Islam and in the spread of Islamic influence to Mediterranean Europe.

After consolidating their position in Spain, the Muslims began to establish institutions of research and learning, whose brilliance was felt far beyond Spain's borders. This was an achievement not of the Arabs alone. It was brought into being by a combination of Africans and Arabs, collectively referred to by Europeans as Moors. The word "Moor" entered the vocabulary of the Europeans meaning "Blacks," as in "blackamoor.")

By the end of the fourteenth century, southern Europe had gained enough strength—military and otherwise—to challenge their African and Arab masters. By the end of the fifteenth century the Arabs and Moors had lost all Spain except the kingdom of Grenada. The Christians, although they also had their internal disputes, were finally united. The marriage of Ferdinand and Isabella joined the formerly hostile royal houses of Aragon and Castile and together their forces blockaded the city of Grenada. After eight months the Moorish governor finally surrendered.

This marked the end of an era. Europe had literally been reborn. The Africans who had planted the seeds of progress in southern Europe had not made the best use of the harvest that followed. The progress and excitement that had inspired Europe during the fifteenth century and had carried medieval Europe over into the modern world had brought no progressive changes to North Africa, now rocked with conflict.

In the countries of North Africa, especially in Morocco, political stagnation seemed to be the general rule, and strong men with selfish intent found their opportunity to seize power. They no longer protected the poets and scholars; they left no monuments to embellish the conquered cities. To North Africans, the fifteenth century was a time in which Spain was a lost and hated land, a century in which Portugal robbed North Africa of a large part of its western seacoast.

The news in 1492 of Christopher Columbus' discovery of the New World came swiftly to the courts of Fez, Marrakesh, and Cairo, and was no cause for rejoicing.

7 Sorrow In A New Land

WHEN IN 1492 COLUMBUS, REPRESENTING THE Spanish monarchy, discovered the New World, he set in train the long and bitter international rivalry over colonial possessions for which, after four and a half centuries, no solution has yet been found. Portugal, which had initiated the movement of international expansion, claimed the new territories on the ground that they fell within the scope of a papal bull of 1455 authorizing her to reduce to servitude all infidel peoples. The two powers, to avoid controversy, sought arbitration and, as Catholics, turned to the Pope—a natural and logical step in an age when the universal claims of the Papacy were still unchallenged by individuals and governments. After carefully sifting the rival claims, the Pope issued in 1493 a series of papal bulls which established a line of demarcation between the colonial possessions of the two states: the East went to Portugal and the West to Spain. The partition, however, failed to satisfy Portuguese aspirations and in the subsequent year the contending parties reached a more satisfactory compromise in the Treaty of Tordesillas, which rectified the papal judgment to permit Portuguese ownership of Brazil."

The above quote from Eric Williams' neo-classic work, *Capitalism and Slavery* (University of North Carolina Press) first published in 1944, places in focus an international situation that started in the latter part of the fifteenth century that is still alive and with us on the eve of the 21st century. Michael Bradley's book, *The Columbus Conspiracy*, is a well-researched inquiry into this event that changed the world for all times to come. This event set in motion the Atlantic slave trade that made possible the economic rise of Europe and the expansion of the influence and domination of European people throughout most of the world.

Christopher Columbus is the best known of a number of Western thugs and murderers who has been presented to the world as a hero and a discoverer. A future examination of his action will prove that he had no regard for the people he encountered on the islands in the Caribbean, and he did not appreciate their initial friendship toward him and his crew.

A fact that is often overlooked is that a large number of the crew of the three vessels of Christopher Columbus were criminals let out of jail to go on this voyage because it was difficult to recruit others because of the apparent danger of such a mission.

The following extracts taken from the *"Journal of the First Voyage of Christopher Columbus, 1492-1493"* (Eric Williams, p. 52) clearly indicate his attitude towards the indigenous people of the Caribbean Islands and the Africans he had previously met. The Portuguese generally referred to the west coast of Africa as "Guinea." It also indicates that Christopher Columbus could have been a participant in the early Portuguese slave trade.

"No. 50 - THE ENSLAVEMENT OF THE ABORIGINAL INDIANS?" (*"Journal of the First Voyage of Christopher Columbus, 1492-1493"*) Friday, 12th of October...They should be good servants and intelligent, for I observe that they quickly took in what was said to them...Sunday, 14th of October...these people are very simple as regards the use of arms, as your Highnesses will see from the seven that I caused to be taken, to bring home and learn our language and return; unless your Highnesses should order them all to be brought to Castile, or to be kept as captives on the same island; for with fifty men they can all be subjugated and made to do what is required of them... Monday, 12th of November...Yesterday a canoe came alongside the ship, with six youths in it. Five came on board, and I ordered them to be detained. They are now here. I afterwards sent to a house on the western side of the river, and seized seven women, old and young, and three children. I did this because the men would behave better in Spain if they had women of their own land, than without them."

The following comment is taken from a speech, "It's Time We Rethink Our History," by David R. Stiddem at the first celebration of African American Culture and History at Stratford High, Nashville, Tennessee and published in *CALC Report*, March 1990, (pp. 6-8).

"When we begin to rethink our history, we understand why history books were wrong. We were all miseducated. Columbus did not discover America. The historical facts: in December, 1492, Columbus was totally lost, wandering around the Caribbean islands thinking he was in Asia, when he was discovered by the native Arawak Americans who lived in these islands. Actually, it was the Arawak's ancestors who, 50,000 years before Columbus, discovered the Americas when they walked across the land bridging the Bering Strait. Columbus didn't discover anything. He was so confused and lost, he thought he was in India, and called the Arawaks "Indians." Christopher Columbus was considered a saint by the European who hailed his great so-called "discovery." We need to rethink our history. Columbus was no saint. And the Arawak were not uncivilized savages. Like the African who came to America before and after Columbus, these were gentle people, with a rich culture, who worshipped the one Creator. When we begin to rethink our history, we begin to put into historical perspective the true role of Europeans in our 500-year history. The prosperity, the wealth the good European life styles we enjoy today in America began in 1492, and from its infant beginnings. This prosperity grew out of slavery. You see, slavery did not begin with the importation of African people to America. Slavery in America began with Columbus. The first slaves were not Africans, but native Americans. Columbus wrote in his journals about the inhabitants of Ayiti (present day Haiti)..."all the inhabitants could be taken away to Castile (Spain), or made slaves on the island. With fifty men, we could subjugate them all and make them do whatever we want." In truth, that is exactly what he did. Columbus enslaved the gentle Arawak Haitians, forced them to give up their gold, and their land. After all, he had "discovered" these riches; they were his for the taking. What is also true is Columbus took hundreds of Arawak slaves to Spain, where they were sold or died; they didn't freely go with Columbus to meet the King, as my history books led us to believe. In his quest for gold, Columbus had the hands cut off of any Arawak who did not bring in his or her quota of gold. In a short 40 years, the entire race of people in Haiti, a half million native Americans, were wiped off the face of the earth by Columbus and the Spaniards that followed him. No, Columbus was no saint. We need to rethink our history."

Non-European people, especially Africans and the Indigenous Americans in the Caribbean Islands referred to as "Indians," initially attributed to the Europeans a humanity and a spirituality that they did not have, and still do not have in their relationship with most of the non-European people of the world. This was a weakness in dealing with the aggressive Europeans, and to some extent it still is. Christopher Columbus was the forerunner of the European aggressor and land-grabber of today. They have justified this action in this regard in the name of God, using the assumption that people were being brought under the influence of civilization. This, indeed, was a contradiction because the act committed against these people was uncivil. When a people assume that their God approves of their criminal action against another people, they have made God ungodly.

In many ways the Europeans' misuse of religion has destroyed the spirituality that was initially the basis of all religion. The Carib and the Arawak Indians were curious about Christopher Columbus and his crew, and at first treated them as strange and new guests in their homes. They did not know that soon after arrival, the guests would turn on the hosts and make them slaves. The destruction of the Caribs and Arawaks in the Caribbean Islands through disease, rape of their women and sometimes out-and-out murder, destroyed the labor supply on these islands and made it a necessity for the Spaniards and other Europeans to create a rationale for the enslavement of the Africans. In his book, *The Disruption of the Indies*, Father de las Casas estimates that from 12 to 25 million Indigenous Americans were killed on the islands in the Caribbean. The school books that indicate that Christopher Columbus was on a civilizing mission are a disservice to students and teachers who should be in rebellion against them.

Christopher Columbus and his crew could have formed a successful partnership with the Indians that would have been to the benefit of both of them. While Christopher Columbus still prevails as a major hero to the Western world, sometime in the not too-distant future, if African and Indian scholars who are descendants of those who were murdered, start writing books about the opening-up of the New World, and start using new and old documents, especially the work of Bartolomeo de las Casas, Christopher Columbus will emerge as one of the great villains of human history, which, indeed, he was. When this revelation becomes apparent to most of the world, I still think there will be a need for Columbus Day but it will be a justifiable day of mourning for the millions of Africans and so-called "Indians" who died to accommodate the spread of European control over the Americas and Caribbean Islands.

Christopher Columbus had helped to set in motion the Atlantic slave trade, the greatest single holocaust in human history.

Most modern day scholars who have a one-dimensional view of history, mostly partial to Europe, are not ready to consider the fact of the pre-Columbian presence of several different national groups before Columbus, going back as far as 1,000 B. C. Professor Ivan Van Sertima's book, *They Came Before Columbus:, The African Presence in Ancient America*, (Random House, New York, 1976), is clear on this subject. The Vikings came in a hurry and obviously left in a hurry. They left little evidence of their culture, of their art and no evidence of their literature. This must have been a culture in transition. The pre-Columbian presence of Orientals in the New Word has been alluded to and partly documented in a number of books, such as *Ancient Egyptians and Chinese in America* by R. A. Jairazbhoy, (Rowman and Littlefield, Totowa, N.J., 1974,) and Columbus was Chinese: *Discoveries and Inventions of the Far East* by Hans Breuer, (Herder and Herder New York, 1972).

This early meeting of the Africans, the Orientals and the Indians was a complementary infusion of culture that today could be a lesson for the whole world because, in all that we have learned in documents, there wasn't even a hint of a war between these cultures and people. This brings us to a conclusion that might be difficult for a lot of people to accept. Maybe the world outside of Europe didn't need the Europeans in the first place. Maybe in this fakery about spreading civilization he destroyed more civilizations than he ever built and did the world more harm than good.

What I learned from reading the literature on this subject is that this early meeting between Indigenous Americans, Orientals and Africans was a laboratory in human relationships because it proved that different people of different cultures and religions and colors can coexist, can complement each other without dominating or attempting to destroy each other. We find the personality of Christopher Columbus and his associates constantly reoccurring in the early part of this drama about the opening of what is referred to as the "New World." Little emphasis is placed on the fact that Christopher Columbus wasn't too clear about where he was and knew nothing about the people he met in the lands he allegedly "discovered." Instead of being a meeting of cultures and an amalgam of cultures complementing each other by infusion, Christopher Columbus set in motion a tragic clash of culture that has not ended to this day. This clash of cultures is caused by the arrogant assumption on the part of some Europeans that they are the only people who ever produced anything worthy of being called a culture.

The following entry in Christopher Columbus' diary is taken from *Documents of West Indian History, Vol. I, 1492-1655: From the Spanish Discovery to the British Conquest of Jamaica*, edited by Eric Williams (p. 4):

"Tuesday, 15th of January...The intercourse at Carib*** would, however, be difficult, because the natives are said to eat human flesh...the Admiral determined to go there, as it was on the route, and thence to Matinino. *** which was said to be entirely peopled by women, without men. He would thus see both islands, and might take some of the natives."

In his entry of 15th of January Christopher Columbus infers that some of the people of Carib (Puerto Rico) are cannibals. This is one of the most persistent myths coming mainly from Europeans using it as a rationale to reduce some non-European people to servitude. This charge is often made and rarely proven. Ironically, the charge of cannibalism is more often charged to a people who in their society have more than an adequate supply of non-human meat. Those making the charge generally come from a society that has been historically short of non-human meat. From this deduction I leave it to the individual reader to arrive at his or her own conclusion.

> Monday, 18th of February....He pretended to have gone over more ground, to mislead the pilots and marines who pricked off the charts, in order that he might remain master of that route to the Indies, as, in fact, he did. For none of the others kept an accurate reckoning, so that no one but himself could be sure of the route to the Indies." (p. 4)

In his entry of 18th of February there is a clear indication of deception between Christopher Columbus and his pilots. If he originally set out to go to the East Indies, why did he go to the West Indies? This is why the Indigenous people, the Caribs and the Arawaks, are referred to as "Indians." This aspect of the Columbus saga begs for investigation over and beyond the Christopher Columbus hero worshippers who have written a library of books about this complex individual who we still do not know.

In Chapter Two of his book, *The Columbus Conspiracy*, Michael Bradley goes beyond the personality of Christopher Columbus and deals with the possibility that there were previous explorers in the Americas, such as the Carthaginians and the Phoenicians. In this speculation Michael Bradley is not only telling us more things that we need to know about early exploration, he is also telling us about human curiosity in relationship to exploration.

In his chapter, *"Echoes of Ancient Truth?"* Michael Bradley alludes to the late development of the nation-state in Europe and the still slower development of a uniform language and culture that Europeans could understand, one to the other. Today, this would seem like a contradiction because in most textbooks and in the mass media, the European is presented to the world as though he arrived culturally pure and endowed with a knowledge and the mandate to lead the world. What Michael Bradley has said in this chapter is that Europeans, like all other people in the world, had to endure a long and hard struggle before arriving at a state and a condition that could justify what is being called "civilization." Europeans lack an understanding of most of the peoples of the world, mainly because they lack an understanding of themselves.

In a previous chapter of this book, Michael Bradley takes up a more dangerous issue. The issue deals with the possible Jewish input into New World discovery and the medieval roots of internal religious conflicts in Europe affecting a segment of the Jewish population who might have disguised themselves as Catholics. He alludes to some misconceptions we might still have about the personality of Jesus Christ, his early life and his relationship to the Jewish people of biblical times. This chapter has both topical and historical roots, putting on the agenda for discussion some little known aspects of the Christian story and its relationship to the role of the Jewish people in world history. This chapter, carefully read, might start debates, fist fights in some places and it might also cause the author, Michael Bradley, to seek a hiding place. Mr. Bradley alludes to the assumption that the Royal House of France could have been Jewish and that the Jewish bloodline came into Europe in this manner.

This information, while generally unknown, has been known and debated by a select group of scholars for the last 40 years. I am of the opinion that these scholars think that people beyond their academic circle are not intelligent enough to understand the truth about history. Michael Bradley has dared to put some forbidden subjects on the agenda for discussion. He has rendered a service that he will not be universally thanked for, but it is a service, nonetheless.

After reading this chapter, I strongly suggest the reading of two very neglected works by Professor Alvin Boyd Kuhn: *Who Is This King of Glory?*, in my opinion one of the clearest books written on the Christ story, and *Shadow of the Third Century*, another ably written book about the early rise of Christianity.

He concludes this chapter with the statement that "Columbus seems to have been born of a heretical family..."

The points that I have been alluding to are summarized by Michael Bradley at the close of Chapter Three:

"Godfroi de Bouillon wanted to create a New Jerusalem in the Holy Land where the three great faiths of the West could be reconciled. He failed, but this sort of crusade is what apparently motivated Christopher Columbus and his supporters and financial backers. His voyage may have been a crusade to establish a 'New Jerusalem in a New World' and, I think, this is the light in which we should view his motivations. It is also a perspective and a light that will permit some insight into the anomalous facts and unlikely coincidences of his life. He seems to have been a part of an ancient, noble conspiracy to create a world of religious toleration between Jew, Christian and Moslem. A New Jerusalem. That, I think, was Columbus' concept of a crusade, and the only worthwhile kind of crusade."

Attempts to unravel the Columbus mystery have not been left to only a few scholars. There has long been debates and some serious questions raised in academic circles without any appreciable public attention being raised. African American scholars, such as J. A. Rogers, Carter G. Woodson and William Leo Hansberry have raised this question in their works. In an essay, "The Origins of Racism in the Americas," by the Caribbean writer, Jan Carew in the book *African Themes: Northwestern University Studies in Honor of Gwendolen M. Carter* (Ibrahim Abu-Lughod, editor, Program of African Studies, Northwestern University, Evanston, Il., 1975, p. 3), he infers that the Columbus exploration to the "New World" was the possible origin of present-day racism. His statement is as follows:

"It is extraordinary that in the 482 years since the Arawakian Lucayos of San Salvador discovered Columbus and his sailors on their beaches, so little research has been done on the origins of racism in the New World. This paucity of research is all the more astonishing when one considers that patterns of race relations and systems of caste, color, and class have not changed a great deal in the four and three-quarter centuries of the Columbian era. But before examining the subject of racism in the New World in Columbian times, we should consider briefly two important early visits to the New World: (1) five centuries before Columbus, Norsemen sailed to Greenland, Labrador, and points south of the St. Lawrence estuary, and (2) in pre-Columbian times Africans visited the Americas, the most notable expedition taking place, Arab chronicles tell us, in 1310, when the emperor of Mali, determined to extend his empire beyond the western reaches of its Atlantic shores, sailed with 400 ships to the New World. The shadowy precursors of both Columbus and the African slave had a distinct bearing on subsequent events and played a significant role in laying the foundations of a new civilization in the Americas."

In Chapter Five of his book, Michael Bradley maintains that there could have been two Columbus's, one being a master pirate of French descent, the other being the Christopher Columbus of history. He points to the documents that made him arrive at his conclusion and the circumstances that tend to prove that the truth of his conclusion is at least a possibility.

In Chapter Six Michael Bradley again alludes to the possible Jewish origins of Christopher Columbus and that the purpose of his voyage had a mission extending beyond discovery and the search for gold. He points to some evidence that tends to indicate a religious meaning for the voyage that is rooted in some of the conflicts and mysteries around the origin of Christianity. Michael Bradley has put on the agenda a subject that might start another crusade, a crusade to kill Michael Bradley in order to shut him up.

To fully understand Michael Bradley's book, it might be necessary to go away from the massive information in the book, new and old, and look at the period in European history from 1400 through 1600. After the Crusades and the period of plagues and famines, Europe had lost one-third of its population. The Africans and the Arabs, who had been controlling Spain in the Mediterranean since the year 711, were still in control, though that control had begun to weaken. Europeans were short of food and the ability to preserve food. They wanted and needed access to the spices, sweets and preservatives of Asia in order to continue to survive. This is the period when some of the conflict between the various factions of the Catholic Church was settled by the marriage of Queen Isabella and Ferdinand of Spain. It was also the period when Spain regained her sovereignty and drove out her Arab and African colonial masters, collectively called "Moors." The Spanish were looking for ethnic and religious purity and therefore expelled the Jews along with the Arabs and the Africans of Moslem faith. This was not only a turning point in the history of Europe, it was a major turning point in the history of the world. This period not only saw the rise of the Atlantic slave trade and the European colonization of most of the world, Europeans subsequently began to colonize information about the history of the world. They colonized complimentary images and began to infer that whiteness was the image of goodness. The most tragic aspect of their colonization of image was their colonization of the image of God and the characters in the Bible. This is the period when the Europeans began to infer that the world was waiting in darkness for Europeans to bring the light. This book has both a historical and a topical meaning that is still very much with us.

Totally aside from opening up the Caribbean Islands, North and South America for European exploration, Christopher Columbus had set in motion the rationale for the destruction of an indigenous population that he mistakenly referred to as "Indians." He had stimulated the Atlantic slave trade. The Africans were used as a rationale to replace the rapidly disappearing "Indian."

8 The Forced Migration

A PROCESS OF CAPTURE AND TRANSPORT WAS SET in motion by the slave trade that changed maritime history, economic history, and created an immigrant population in the Caribbean Islands and in the Americas, who were forced out of their homes against their will. The basis of this force was the need and greed of Europe. Their forced migration was a process that ignored the humanity of a large portion of humankind. This process, set in motion during the latter part of the fifteenth century, would last over 300 years until slavery was turned into colonization, a more sophisticated form of slavery.

There is a need now to look at this process and how it was set in motion. Most of the information used for this examination is taken from the article, *African Slave Trade, The Cruelest Commerce* (September 1992, National Geographic) by Colin Palmer, Professor of History at the University of North Carolina at Chapel Hill, from Basil Davidson's *Black Mothers: The Years of the African Slave Trade* and A. Adu Boahen's*The Coming Of the Europeans (Horizon History of Africa)*. To set the process in motion, the African was totally dehumanized in the minds of the Europeans. So far as most of them were concerned, the Africans were outside of the grace of God; Africans became living commodities in a world trade system that laid the basis for modern capitalism. The Middle Passage, the condition of the transfer of the Africans across the Atlantic to the various ports of embarkation where they were to be sold as slaves, is the most tragic story of forced migration in human history.

Europe took full advantage of wars and conflicts between West African tribes and nations and began to purchase some of the captives and prisoners of war as slaves. The kind of slavery that the European was about to introduce into West Africa had no relationship to the African system of indentured servitude. In the African system the slave was usually a loser in a local war. He was not enslaved separate from his family and no slave was sent outside of Africa. Some slaves with talent rose to be kings in the very house in which they had been slaves. The word slave in West Africa had an entirely different meaning than it had when used by the Europeans. The slave in Africa did not lose her/his humanity. Some African chiefs or kings became corrupt and went into the slave trade because they wanted to. The Europeans sold firearms to one African group to either protect themselves or capture another group. The European gunpowder, rum and cheap bric-a-brac coming from the embryo of what will eventually become the European Industrial Revolution, was traded for slaves.

In every slave fort in West Africa, there is a door of no return. The captured slaves went out of this door to the beach and subsequently to the boats that would take them away from their home forever. The condition on these boats was beyond anything described in a concentration camp or in a chain gang in the South of the 1920's and 1930's.

Professor Colin Palmer described the condition and the establishment of these slave holding forts in the following manner:

"To facilitate trade, forts were established along the West African coast. The Gold Coast (contemporary Ghana) saw construction of more than 50 such posts along 300 miles of coastline. The larger forts were called castles. Among the best known, Elmina Castle in Ghana was built by the Portuguese in 1482 but fell to the Dutch in 1637. Cape Coast Castle, begun by the Swedes in 1653, was later held by the dey, or ruler, of the Fetu people, it was acquired by the Dutch in 1664 and by the English in 1665. This castle could accommodate more than a thousand slaves."

Professor Palmer further informs us that:

"The Atlantic passage tested bodies and souls to their limits. The human cargoes were arranged on wooden platforms 'like books on a shelf' on various levels in the cramped hold. Rarely was there space for an adult to stand erect. Some had barely enough room to lie down. One ship's surgeon observed that the traders" wedged them in so that they had not so much room as a man in his coffin either in length or breadth. It was impossible for them to turn or shift with any degree of ease. Some traders, of course, realized that such crowding increased the incidence of disease and death. One agent of the Royal African Company complained in 1704 of inadequate space on the ship 'Postillion': 'The slaves are so large, [and] it being the general opinion that the slaves could not be healthy in the space of three foot, they broke up one of the platforms which was the reason she couldn't carry more than 100 slaves.' Eight years later the company advised its agents at Cape Coast Castle: 'Pray lade no more than are necessary to prevent Mortality which has often happened by crowding the ship with too many Negroes.' Not until the 18th century did European countries engaged in the trade set standards for the allocation of space to the slaves; it may be doubted whether the rules were obeyed. Fearing rebellion, ships' crews generally chained the slaves securely in the hold, usually in pairs, the right ankle of one connected to the left ankle of the other. James Penny, who commanded trading vessels for more than 20 years, recounted that when no danger 'is apprehended, their fetters are by degrees taken off.' With so many bodies closely packed together, the heat below-decks became unbearable. The air reeked of excrement and infected sores. By the 18th century, ships customarily had portholes to aid ventilation, 'windsails to throw down a current of air and gratings on the decks.' But to the human cargo, the hold remained a fetid hell."

A cruel philosophical argument developed among the slave traders, between the concept of tight pack and loose pack. When the slaves were tightly packed on the ship, more could be loaded on but more died. In loose pack, more survived the journey because they had breathing space because fewer slaves were packed on the ship. Therefore, when slaves arrived at the port of debarkation they were in a healthier condition. The argument would go on for another 100 years.

There is a small library of literature on the Middle Passage, some written by captains of slave ships. The rationale and the pretense in England was that the slave was primitive, un-Christian, and that slavery brought them under the tutelage of Christianity. Other slave trading nations took the same attitude. The best literature illustrating this rationale came from the Catholic and the Protestant Church.

It is time that we look, at least briefly, at slavery and what is referred to as the New World and how it developed.

9 The Slave Trade In The New World

THE AFRICANS WERE NO STRANGERS TO THE NEW WORLD; they seem to have been in North America and South America long before Columbus. This is more than an assumption, thanks to the research of Professor Leo Weiner, reported in his *Africa and the Discovery of America*, and the work of Harold G. Lawrence in another book called *African Explorers to the New World*.

The first Africans who came to the New World were not in bondage, contrary to popular belief. Africans participated in some of the early expeditions, mainly with Spanish explorers. The best-known of these African explorers was Estevanico, sometimes known as Little Steven, who accompanied the de Vaca expedition during six years of wandering from Florida to Mexico. The remarkable thing about Estevanico, who came to America in 1527, is that he was a remarkable linguist. He learned the language of the Indians in a matter of weeks. Because of his knowledge of herbs and medicines, he was accepted as a deity by some Indian tribes.

In 1539, Estevanico set out from Mexico in a party with Fray Marcos de Niza in search of the fabulous Seven Cities of Cibola. When most of the expedition, including Fray Marcos, became ill, Estevanico went on alone and opened up what is now known as New Mexico and Arizona.

A number of historians have stated that Pedro Nino, one of the pilots of the command ship of Christopher Columbus, was an African. In the discovery of the Pacific in 1513, Balboa carried thirty Africans, who helped to clear the road across the isthmus between the two oceans. In the conquest of Mexico, Cortez was accompanied by a number of Africans. Incidentally, one was a pioneer of wheat farming in the New World.

In the exploration of Guatemala, Chile, Peru, and Venezuela, Africans arrived nearly a hundred years before they reappeared as slaves in Jamestown, Virginia, in 1619.

Thus, Africans were major contributors to the making of the New World, and they did not come culturally empty-handed. Many of the Africans brought to the New World such skills as iron working, leather working and carpentry.

Before the breaking up of the social structure of the West African states such as Ghana and Songhai, and the internal strife that made the slave trade possible, many Africans, especially West Africans, lived in a society in which university life was fairly common and scholars were held in reverence.

In that period in Western African history, the university of Sankore at Timbuktu was flourishing, and its great chancellor, the last of the monumental scholars of West Africa, Ahmed Baba reigned over that university. A great African scholar, he wrote 47 books, each on a separate subject. He received all of his education within Africa; in fact, he did not leave the Western Sudan until he was exiled to Morocco during the invasion in 1594.

My point is this: There existed in Africa prior to the beginning of the slave trade a cultural way of life that in many ways was equal, if not superior, to many of the cultures then existing in Europe. And the slave trade destroyed these cultures and created a dilemma that the African has not been able to extract himself from to this day.

There were, in the Africans' past, rulers who extended kingdoms into empires, great armies that subdued entire nations, generals who advanced the technique of military science, scholars with wisdom and foresight, and priests who told of gods that were kind and strong. But with the bringing of the African to the

New World, every effort was made to destroy his memory of having ever been part of a free and intelligent people.

The greatest destroyer of African culture, the greatest exploiter of the African, was the plantation system of the New World. The African was transformed into something called a Negro. He was demeaned. This is the thing that is uniquely tragic about the African slave system. Of all the slave systems in the world, no other dehumanized the slave more than that started by the Europeans in the fifteenth century. Using the church as a rationale, they began to set up myths that nearly always read the African out of human history, beginning with the classification of the African as a lesser being. The Catholic Church's justification for slavery was that the African was being brought under the guidance of Christendom and that he would eventually receive its blessings.

The rationale was that slavery was a blessing to the African. It was not.

There were several competing slave systems in the New World. In order to understand the effects of these various systems on the personality of the Africans, we have to look at each one individually. In Cuba and Haiti, often the Africans were a majority in the population. This is also true of certain portions of Brazil. Therefore the system operated differently in these areas, and, although it was still slavery, the African had some cultural mobility.

In South America and in the West Indies, the slave master did not outlaw the African drum, African ornamentations, African religion, or other things dear to the African, remembered from his former way of life. This permitted a form of cultural continuity among the slaves in the West Indies, Cuba, and South America that did not exist in the United States.

In the Portuguese area, in the West Indies, and often in South America, the plantation owner would buy a shipload or half a shipload of slaves. These slaves usually came from the same areas in Africa, and they naturally spoke the same language and had the same basic culture. Families, in the main, were kept together. If a slave on an island was sold to a plantation owner at the other end of the island, he could still walk to see his relatives.

This made for a form of cultural continuity among the slaves in South America, Cuba, and Haiti that later made their revolts more successful than revolts in the United States.

In the United States, in the fight to destroy every element of culture of the slaves, the system was cruel. No other system did so much to demean the personality of the slave, to deny his personality, or to ruthlessly sell family members away from each other. The American slave system operated almost like the American brokerage system. If a person bought twenty slaves at the beginning of the week, and found himself short of cash at the end of the week, he might, if the price was right, sell ten. These men might be resold within a few days. The family, the most meaningful entity in African life, was systematically and deliberately destroyed. But in South America, the slave managed to stay in his group and therefore preserved some of his cultural continuity.

In spite of these drastic drawbacks, the Africans in the Americas, including the United States, made a meaningful contribution to the preservation of the countries in which he was a slave.

Another neglected aspect of the African in the New World is the role of the African women. Comparatively few White women were brought to the New World during the first hundred years. Many families of the New World originated from cohabitation between the White slave master and the African woman. Later, this same slave master, especially in the United States, made and supported laws forbidding his own child to have an education or sit beside him on public transportation. In Haiti, the African woman sometimes had a kind of semi-legal status. In South America, especially in Brazil, sometimes the White slave master married the African woman and she became a free person. These free African women in South America began to maneuver their husbands in an attempt to lessen the harshness of the slave system. In the United States, however, there could be no such maneuver.

Haiti and Cuba, during this early period, were dominated by their "mother countries." Wars were started within these countries to liberate them from their European masters. Africans made a meaningful contribution toward the early liberation of Cuba, Haiti and other areas of South America; they fought with Simon Bolivar for the freedom of South America, and fought valiantly to free Haiti from the domination of the French.

In the United States, especially in the American Revolution, the African slave often took the place of a White person, who decided that he did not want to fight, and fought with the promise that he would get his freedom afterward. Thousands of Africans fought in the American Revolution with this promise. And, a little-known incident in our history is that thousands of Africans fought with the British when the British made the same promise and the African believed them. Apparently it depended on who got to him first.

The African was a major contributor in the making of the New World; the economy of the New World rested largely on slave labor. For many years, one-third of the trade of the New World was with the small island of Santo Domingo, which later became Haiti. Haiti and the other Caribbean islands also influenced the economic system of Europe.

Slavery and the slave trade was the first international investment in capital. It was the first large-scale investment that was intercontinental. Many Europeans invested in ships and in the goods and services taken from these African countries and became independently wealthy.

But the slave revolts continued. By the end of the seventeenth century, the picture of slavery began to change drastically. Economic necessity, not racial prejudice, originally directed the African slave trade to the New World. As early as 1663, a group of slaves joined a group of White indentured servants in a revolt. Some slaves took the Christian version of the Bible literally and believed that God meant for them to be free men—slaves such as Gabriel Prosser in Virginia, who led a revolt of 40,000 slaves in 1800. In 1822 in Charleston, South Carolina, a carpenter, Denmark Vesey planned one of the most extensive slave revolts on record, but he was betrayed and put to death with many of his followers. And in 1831, Nat Turner led the greatest slave revolt ever to occur in Virginia.

The slaves never accepted their condition passively. In his book, *American Negro Slave Revolts*, Dr. Herbert Aptheker records 250 slave revolts.

The African slave in the Americas, in addition to assisting in the freedom and the economy of these countries, made a major contribution to his freedom.

In the story of the rise and fall of great African states, and subsequently the slave trade, we are trying to deal with something much bigger than history itself. We are trying to deal with an old situation and a new situation and trying to address ourselves to the current cry for Black history and Black power.

Our major point is this: The African people who became slaves in the United States have been many things in history, good and bad. They have ruled great nations and they have destroyed great nations. They are profoundly human. And they have played every role in the human drama, from saint to buffoon. Slavery does not represent the sum total of our history.

We are searching for a definition of our African heritage and to determine what it means to a people emerging from bondage into the light of freedom, reentering the mainstream of world history as participants.

A good definition of heritage, or history, is: Heritage is something acquired or transmitted by a predecessor. It is also called a "legacy," "tradition," and "birthright." But when we speak of our people, perhaps a new and better definition is in order.

In his book *Tom Tom*, John Vandercook said, "A race is like a man. Until it uses its own talent, takes pride in its own history and loves its own memories, it can never fulfill itself completely." Heritage, in essence, is how a people have used their talents to command the respect of other people. The ultimate purpose of our heritage and heritage teaching is to show our people how, through identity and through respect for themselves, they can work to liberate themselves from the old ties of bondage. A person's relationship to his heritage, after all, is the same as the relationship of a child to its mother.

10 The Broader Dimensions of the Crisis

I HAVE NO GREAT FEELING FOR THE JAPANESE and the new yellow racism that is developing among them, but I have some admiration for the way they recovered from defeat and dealt with their conqueror. They never let their mind forget the nature of their defeat, who defeated them and how. They knew — without shouting, without holding a single mass meeting — that their enemy threw two atomic bombs on their nation. They have figuratively and literally asked the question: If the Japanese were one of the two main enemies you had in war, why did you throw two bombs on the Japanese instead of one on each enemy? In the rise of their own racism, they have properly interpreted the racism of those who defeated them militarily but not commercially. The assumption is that they threw two on you because you were not White. They imprison your people because you are not White. The Japanese refused to let their enemy take away from them their self-confidence and their idea of God as they conceived God to be. If a people can hold on to that, you can recover from almost anything.

Now let's end by saying what we could have done to recover from the disaster of the world Christopher Columbus did not discover. During the concept of Caribbean Federation, the first thing we should have done was to unify all of those islands and have a common defense force. Therefore, there would have been no Grenada and no Panama invasion. There would have been a common currency, a common defense force, an economic union—what one couldn't produce, the other could produce—a common tax structure. Put them all together and look at all the territory you've got once you've developed a common unity and a common parliament.

Every state in the United States has its own state legislature and local representation. Yet every state in the United States has representation in Washington. So having a common parliament for all of the Caribbean Islands does not keep them from having local things specifically to take care of local situations as well as having a common parliament to take care of island-wide situations.

We have not dealt with the contradictions. The concept of Pan Africanism was created by three Trinidadians: (1) H. Sylvester Williams (2) C. L. R. James and (3) George Padmore. Why is it that they could never unify Trinidad or a single island? The mission of Pan Africanism was to unify the survivors of our Holocaust that Christopher Columbus and his associated European thugs set in motion.

The Japanese sent their children to the leading schools of the world to learn all the necessary skills and bring them home. Are there any foreigners building their airplanes or building their ships? They do it themselves. When you have to call your former master back to do basic things for you, you are not free you have re-enslaved or recolonized yourself. We spend too much time celebrating, too much time with our fists in the air, too much time talking about Black power (without having any of it).

Alton Maddox has said the Civil Rights movement was a consumer rights movement, and indeed it was. We were fighting to consume somebody else's hamburger. We made White hotels rich by having our conferences there. All of the conferences that Black people have each year would allow us to build ten major hotels at once. We could employ each other. Looking at all the empty land doing nothing we could have a series of farms scattered over every state. We could raise our own food; it would be much better if we could stop eating out of the can all the time. We know what comes out of the ground. We've a brother putting it in the ground; a brother taking it out and a brother putting it on the truck. Look how many people you are employing. What did we lose everywhere? The concept of nation responsibility. This is what has been taken away from us during these five hundred years. This is the supreme tragedy on our mind in the world Christopher Columbus did not discover, programming our mind to convince us that we could not even make a safety pin. If you can't make a safety pin, you can't make a locomotive.

We have to tabulate how many years we're going to be dependent on other people for basic survival. The bargaining chip, sooner or later, will be I will close off your community and let nothing come in...then what are you going to do? Not only have you not learned how to make a gun, you haven't learned how to fix one. All of these veterans coming out of the Army, with all this skill...have you learned how to marshal that skill, and how to tap that skill? These veterans could have gone to Africa and built some of the finest armies in the world. I have often said, "The Black man properly equipped, properly inspired, and properly led is the greatest human fighting machine the world has ever known." However, our skill has always gone to fighting for other people. Let's go to Africa itself.

There are Africans educated in Africa with African money who are scattered all over the world; they want to be everything but Africans. They have turned Africa over to a bunch of thugs. Coup after coup after coup. Who is going to give Africa the stability that it needs? I maintain—and this might be away from the subject—that there is no solution for African people, except for some form of Pan African Nationalism, no matter how you cut it. No matter what island you're from, no matter what state you're from, no matter what religion you belong to...we must develop a concept of our Pan Africanism that cuts across all religious, political, social, fraternity, sorority lines and allows us to proudly face the world as one people.

We must stop apologizing, stop imitating and begin to innovate. For a people to be free, they have to produce one sacrificial generation. That generation must be the role model for other generations to come. Maybe a generation will have to wear dungarees so that another generation can wear tuxedos. We haven't yet considered that.

We have to seriously step back and think of what we need to do and how do we liberate ourselves from the plagues, cultural famines and misconceptions set in motion by the rise of Europe during the Christopher Columbus period of the fifteenth and sixteenth centuries. How do we become a whole people again? I think we should begin by finding a mirror and liking what we see. If we can't like what we see, then we can't make each other whole again. It can't be just ceremony; we can't just decorate the outside of the head forever without putting something inside of the head.

We can't have war between men and women because no people can be free if one half of the mind of the people is tied up in conflict. It's going to have to be both of us, or none of us. We're going to have to find some unity that stretches across ideology lines, cultural lines, accent lines and national lines. We're hung up with so many off-beat religions—none of which we created— we're cutting each other to pieces, deserting each other, destroying each other based on ideologies of no consequence to us as a people.

I remember as a little boy on a farm, I was churning until the butter comes to the top. I'm counting the churns and I asked my Great Grandmother, "Which one of the churns brings up the butter?" "All of them my son," she said. "Which one?" "No one...all of them." We have to realize it is not the effort of any one of us that will lead to freedom, but the collective work of all of us who are sincere. That will ultimately end in the freedom and liberation of our own people and the indoctrination of our own children so that they in turn will pick up the responsibility and create an age where you never have to call for freedom again because there will never be any need to call for it. From that day forward we'll always have it. This is our mission and, in turn, the legacy that we need to leave for our children and the still more beautiful ones not yet born.

Our enslavement and the wreck and ruin of the sovereign states of Africa started at the beginning of the Colonial Era. Our enslavement and the rape of the services of our countries helped to lay the basis of present-day capitalism. Again the Europeans have squandered their wealth on stupid wars and conflicts that could have been avoided. They have already proven that they have one mission in mind, irrespective of religion, politics or cultural affiliation and that mission is to dominate the world and all of its resources by any means necessary. The new rationale for this dominance is now called a New World Order. All African and other non-European people should be on the alert, because a new form of slavery could be more brutal and more sophisticated than the slavery of the Christopher Columbus Era.

Africans and other non-European people must plan and strategize for a New World Order distinctly their own that will be developed by them, for them. Our mission should be not to conquer Europe, but to contain Europe within its borders and let it be known that anything Europe wants from other parts of the world can be had through honorable trade.

If we understand our mission, I think we will become aware of the fact that we are in a position to give the world a new humanity that will bring into being a new world of safety and respect for all people.

The Nile River civilizations of Africa gave the world its first humanity, its first belief systems, its first social thought and its first philosophy. With the restoration of self-confidence we need to say to ourselves, "If we did it once, we can do it again."

11 When Will We Memorialize The Victims of Our Holocaust

IT IS UNFORTUNATELY FORGOTTEN THAT during slavery, and colonialism, Africa and its people suffered the greatest loss in population and cultural devastation of any people in history. There is no memorial calling attention to this event any place in all the world. The Africans in Africa have not properly memorialized their loss and the Africans outside of Africa, the major victims of slavery and colonialization, have erected no edifices or monument to remind their children that some of them survived the greatest protracted crime in history. I maintain that the people of the entire African world, both in Africa and abroad, are delinquent in their responsibility to their ancestors until some proper memorials are erected in every place in the world where there is an African population.

This subject is so big that it is frightening. I wonder why a people as large as we are, engaged in as many activities as we are engaged in, have waited so long to think of addressing ourselves to the subject: The Middle Passage, Our Holocaust! It is our holocaust because this is a holocaust that started 500 years ago and it is not over. We do not start our count at 6 million, we start counting at 60 million, and we have just begun to count. Now, I do not mean to negate the German and the European holocaust.

Whether the number was 6 or 60 million, even if it was 3 million, it was wrong. But it was a problem started in Europe by Europeans. There is no comparison between this tragedy and our tragedy which was the greatest single crime in the history of the world. Why haven't we memorialized our dead? It was almost like the crime of not burying them!

Let's look at it historically, broadside, before we come to the subject. Why are we, a people whom so many have said have no history, pursued by so many other people? Why is it that we have been a prize to be captured down through the years? It is because of a prevailing thing that prevails right now. African people have been under siege for over 3,000 years for the same reason they are under siege right now: African people have always had and still have something other people want, think they can't do without, and don't want to pay for! You keep using the word "apartheid" about South Africa. It is a minor issue in comparison to the real issue. The real issue in South Africa is a form of economic slavery. It is Western domination of the mineral wealth of South Africa and subsequently the mineral wealth of the whole world. The assault on South Africa, the assault on Africa in general, is an assault on the gold in the Western Sudan and there lies the major gold wealth of Africa. Except for it, the economic system under which you live would not be the same or even reasonably the same.

Let us go to the background of the tragedy because very often, you think that this happened quite by accident. Let's set the stage for what happened. It is too big for literature. Let's put it in the realm of theater. It was a world drama. A tragedy. And it started inside of the European mind. Let us look at the 200-year turning point in world history, 1400 to 1600 A.D. Let's look at where Europe was. Europe had just finished the period of the Crusades, one of the great phony charades of human history. It had nothing to do with religion; it was a political move to divert the attention of Europe from the fact that the Church had played so many games on the people that the people were about to explode and destroy it. So they found an issue to divert the people's attention from that fact. Once they started them to marching and going to rescue the Holy Grail (which wasn't even lost in the first place), they would forget that they had been bled dry to build all those cathedrals so that all the priests and monks could live in luxury while most of the population of Europe lived in poverty. They would forget that Europeans had, to a great extent, enslaved Europeans. Feudalism was still rampant in Europe. Now, to divert their attention, they needed an issue. The Crusades, the rescue of the Holy Grail, and the fight against the hated infidel became that great issue.

The Africans and the Arabs had blocked the European's entry to the Mediterranean since 711 A.D., when the African general Tarik Bin Ziad had conquered Spain. It was an African-Arab partnership. Now, when the Arabs write history, they leave out the Africans, and when the Europeans write, they leave out the Africans. So, therefore, if you want to get in the story, you write the story. We're at the end of this dominance, the great flourishing period of scientific discovery. You assume that when Europe was having its Middle Ages, everyone else was having theirs. There were people in the world who had no Middle Age, no age of backwardness, no feudalism, and those people were in Africa, Inner West Africa, the Western Sudan. Three great, magnificent African states, Ghana, Mali, Songhai unfolded while Europe was having its period of depression The last of these states was now reaching the apex of its grandeur. In 1415 the Portuguese attacked a part of Morocco, a little place called Cueta, and for the first time a European had taken over some African territory. This put heart in Europe because they had at last invaded the territory of what they considered to be the hated infidel. At this juncture of history everyone not of your chosen religion was considered to be an infidel. The European Christian called the Arab infidel, and the Arabs called the Christian infidel. They had been capturing each other in the Mediterranean, but for the first time the European Christian had taken some land from the African.

In 1450, the Africans and the Arabs were having an argument in Spain, and this argument was weakening their hold on Spain. In 1455 Spain and Portugal had gained enough freedom from African-Arab domination of the Mediterranean to go to the pope to seek arbitration, because now they were getting colonial ambitions of their own. They said: Once we are free of Moorish domination, what are we going to do? They were now talking about what part of the world they were going to take. The pope, settling the argument, said: You are both authorized to reduce to servitude all infidel people. He issued a papal bull to this effect. I'm assuming that some of you have read Eric Williams' book, *Capitalism and Slavery*. This event is well documented in other books, but best done in *Capitalism and Slavery*.

Europe is awakening from its own lethargy. Prince Henry, called Henry the Navigator, although there was no evidence that he ever went to sea, finds a cache of maps. The maps were used by Jewish gold dealers in the Western Sudan. The Jews had access to the Western Sudan before anyone else and in preference to others. This is another lecture, for another day. But for over 3,000 years, people called Hebrews, or Jews, have been given preferred treatment over other people, a fact which they have never acknowledged to this day. They were given preferred treatment in the trade of gold in the Western Sudan and they were the major gold dealers between Spain, the Mediterranean states, and the nations in Africa called the Western Sudan. They had made maps of the areas going into the Western Sudan and these are some of the maps that Henry the Navigator got a hold of to start his school of chart making and map making. Europe had lost the concepts of longitude and latitude. But they learned from the information gathered in Spain and preserved by the Africans and the Arabs, collectively called the Moors, at the University of Salamanca. There were only two great universities in the whole world at the time, Salamanca in Spain, and Sankore at Timbuktu. There was no Harvard, now, no Cambridge, no Oxford; none of these schools were in existence. Two universities in the whole world, one solely manned by Africans, Sankore at Timbuktu, one partly manned by Africans, Salamanca in Spain. They had translated the maritime information coming out of China, the leading maritime nation of the world of that day. With maritime knowledge, the European goes out to sea.

The Africans have also preserved the intellectual masters of Europe, Plato, Aristotle, and Socrates, as well as some of the basis of European Christianity. The Europeans would now use that information and turn on the people who had preserved it. No one, but no one has ever sent us a thank-you note for anything we ever did for them which makes us a totally unobligated people. We owe no one anything, politically left or right. Everybody who has come among us has taken away more than they brought, and more than they gave. We have been humane to all the people we have met. No one ever fought their way into Africa. They came as guests and stayed as conquerors or slave traders.

With Europeans beginning to see the light, they start looking for something to replenish their empty bowls. They are coming out of the lethargy of the Middle Ages. They have survived famines and plagues and lost one-third of their population. They are looking for the spices and sweets of the East. They were not looking for Africa at first. They were looking for something to put on that gosh-darn awful European food so they could eat it, and they discovered Africa, en route. They discovered a richer prize while seeking a route to the east, and they captured this prize instead of pursuing the route to Asia. They would get to Asia and find Asia more politically sophisticated because the Asians were accustomed to conquerors and visitors with no good intentions. Europe would have to deal with the Asians in a different way. The Asians would have invited them to dinner, but they would have watched them through the dinner and if they suspected that they had evil intentions, they might have slipped something into the food. But the Africans were generous and that's why they were trapped.

The Portuguese began to come down the coast of Africa in 1438, but didn't begin to take slaves out of Africa until 1442. Their taking of slaves out of Africa started with a misunderstanding of African internal servitude which was based on the extraction of labor after war captivity. Many times Africans captured in internal wars, sometimes just skirmishes, had to work so many months or years as penalty for losing the war. There were no great casualties. After serving their period of indenture they would go free. You lost a war, and that was what you had to do. Once there was an accumulation of labor over and above that which could be used locally, since the Africans had no massive transportation, they began to use Portuguese ships to lend that labor to other kings or chiefs further down the coast. The Portuguese interpreted this as Africans enslaving other Africans, and subsequently used this as a rationale to do the same thing. The role of the Africans in the slave trade is still being misinterpreted by Africans, African-Americans, and especially, White scholars who are not scholarly enough to understand that the Africans could not have possibly managed or set in motion anything as massive as the three-continent industry of the Western slave trade.

Let us look at this turning point in history, this 200-year turning point, with Europe coming out of the Middle Ages and relearning the skill of shipping. Europe, having lost its sentimental attachment to itself and that of other people, then began to explode. We must look at the world after 1492, but even before that there's a date you have to reconsider, 1482, when an expedition sailed down the coast of West Africa and demanded to build a fortress at Elmina. In this grouping of ships were sailors and soldiers waiting off-shore, for, if the king didn't buy the Bible story, he'd have to buy the gun story. The Portuguese forced their way in and built the first permanent fortification, Elmina Castle the largest slave-holding fortress in all West Africa. In this expedition was a little-known sailor, Cristobal Colon, later known as Christopher Columbus. He said in his diary: "As man and boy, I sailed up and down the Guinea coast for 23 years." What was he doing up and down the Guinea coast for 23 years? He was obviously in the early Portuguese slave trade. This is why once he and his disease-ridden men had almost destroyed the Caribs and the Arawaks, whom he mistakenly called Indians, he himself suggested bringing Africans to replace them. He had asked Father de las Casas to go to Rome to get sanction of the Church to do so, and this Father de las Casas did. Of course, near the end of his life, Father de las Casas said that it was wrong to enslave the African as well as the Indian. That was 35 years later. The Indians were dead, and some of the Africans were dead.

What I'm trying to look at is that the war on the African started before he got on the ship. This was a war waged on the structure of African society, especially the family, in that the attack on the Black male started right there and it continues to this day "The Color Purple" was not a movie, it was continuation of that war. You might have looked at it for entertainment, but that was not entertainment. It was propaganda as skillfully put as the propaganda that came out of Nazi Germany. More skillful, because Blacks participated in it and rationalized about it and said it was art.

I've gone through these slave forts, most of the major ones. I went through Goree, the slave fort in the French area, and that's the third time I've gone through that one within the year. If you look at the structure you see that it was designed so that the slave sellers lived in luxury over the slave dungeons below. Upon the onset of evening, the women would be assembled in the courtyard so that the captains could pick out the one they wanted to violate that night, and these Africans had not even left Africa yet. We see the beginning of a process which we have not dealt with as a people: bastardization when they not only bastardized the body, they bastardized the mind. Today you can find a jet-black person with a bastardized mind. He doesn't know where his mind is, or who he's loyal to, or who his paymaster is. But that process of physical bastardization would begin there, and part of the mental bastardization would also begin there, because sometimes they kept back the mother and the bastard child and they would later become part of the slave trade system in the village around the fort. But now, once the system got underway and the people were on their way to the various markets, we have another process, which is the same process in a slightly different way.

This is a tragedy of such proportion that it taxes the imagination and some Blacks want to forget about it, and maybe this is why we have not memorialized our dead. This constitutes the greatest number of unmemorialized people in the history of the whole world. No other people have permitted that many of their people to die and have not attempted to make a suitable memorial for them. I say again, it's like having not buried them. It's like they are still there, like their voices are still there. They have left us with something. I remember speaking to Ray Charles once, and I was trying to explain the particular nature of the genius in his voice, and he didn't get the point and I was kind of sorry that I had put it that way. I said, "Ray, the particular genius in your voice is that of protracted crying. That's the wail and the crying in those slave ships coming back down through the genes, and through the years." He shook his head and said, "Where did you get this crazy cat? I wish I could see him." He missed the point. I had never been more sincere in all my life. And I believe that the genius of our survival is what we have misunderstood.

When we discuss the numbers lost in this trade, we are in an endless discussion of how many, and that depends on who you are listening to. If 20 million cleared through Goree, that's just one fortress and not even the largest one. Twenty million cleared through that one place, and Goree was late in getting started, and the monster, the largest of the slave forts, was at Elmina Castle, whose dungeons could hold over a thousand at one time. Let's put these together. Another figure to add is that of those lost in the movement from the hinterlands to the coast. Sometimes seven out of ten got lost. Sometimes slave catchers, in competition with each other, or just for meanness and spite, killed each other's captives. That means that 100% got lost, 10 out of 10 got lost. Now these are statistics that didn't get in anyone's computer. Some of the slave captains were thieves and cheats working for absentee slave owners. They would load, say 350 slaves on a ship, list in their log 300, stop at a port and sell 50, and put the proceeds directly in their pocket. These statistics got lost. These statistics didn't get into anyone's computer, but the money got into their pockets. I'm saying that nearly every figure that you hear could be absolutely wrong, or could be partly right. But if it's a low figure, it is fully wrong.

But understand what is happening now. There was no resource in all the world that Europe could get to rebuild its financial structure after the Middle Ages. The economy of Europe was rebuilt on the slave trade. That except for this trade, the economy of Europe would not have pulled out of the depression of the Middle Ages, except for us and except for what was extracted from us. It did not start on its way to recovery in the United States, because the United States, in this early period, did not exist. The recovery started in the exploitation of the plantation system of the Caribbean Islands.

How the people got there was a double miracle because a question arose between the slave sellers and shippers over "tight pack" versus "loose pack." If they packed the slaves tight, we're talking about the Middle Passage itself, how, if they packed them tight in the ship, through suffocation, large numbers of them would die. From one-third to one-half wouldn't reach the market. But if they packed them loose, they'd have enough breathing space that a goodly number of them would live through the ordeal and get to the market. So, the argument became: is it more economic to loose pack or tight pack? No one was talking about or thinking about Africans as human beings. Sometimes the sickly and the rebellious were just thrown overboard. The total dehumanization is what has to be looked at.

In the establishment of South America and the Caribbean Islands, something happened there that didn't happen in the United States. The slavemasters bought in large lots and kept the lots together. They thought they could work them better that way. They were right. But they forgot—the Africans could revolt better that way. They maintained cultural continuity to a great extent because they came from the same general area in Africa. They could speak the same language, and if you sold grandma, or grandpa, or uncle to someone on the other side of the island, they could walk to the other side of the island and see their relatives once in a while. There was a language that all of them understood and that was the language of the drum. In the United States, they outlawed all African instruments, and African religion, and this left the African in the United States without anything other than mental recall. Here they bought in small lots and broke those lots up. When people do that they break up the African loyalty system. We suffer to this day because they broke our loyalty system. This breakage caused the creation of a cleavage between the field Black and the house Black—that's what Malcolm X was trying to explain. Now you can understand why in South America and in the Caribbean, many slave revolts were planned and executed by house servants, while in the United States, many of them were betrayed by house servants. It has nothing to do with which one of those people were braver than the other. By breaking our culture continuity, they broke the line of loyalty—one to the other. We look at those people in the house and we say: we don't know what tribe he came from, he didn't come from my tribe, I can tell by the scars on his face he didn't come from my tribe, so I don't have any loyalty to him. He's up there eating food in the house while I'm out here eating this coarse food in the field, I don't have any feeling towards him. Who is he? But the man in the field in the Caribbean and the one in the house, can tell by the speech and by the look of the other that they came from the same basic area in Africa and possibly from the same group. Caribbeans misunderstand this to this day—most Black Americans never knew it. But we have got to study both. I studied it several ways, and I say if we're ever going to effect some kind of unity, understand that we've got to look at all of the Africans who were brought here. And we will have to pay some special attention to those in South America, especially Brazil where the largest number exist today. They did more with African culture continuity and with the consistency of it than any Africans in the New World including Haiti. Did more with it by establishing two African states in Brazil, Bahia and Palmyras, one of which lasted 110 years.

What I am trying to show is that in a collective way through the Africans in the Middle Passage, and through what was extracted from them, an economy came into being and that economy made possible the modern technical and scientific world of the West. That world that was built on our sweat and our labor and our death now says what we cannot do when they struck at Africa, when Africa was on the verge of a pre-industrial age. We will never know what Africa could have been because they struck while Africa was growing. The internal differences between African state and African state were far less than some internal differences between European state and European state right now.

But the African suffered from a kind of naiveté he is still suffering from. He permitted Europeans to arbitrate his family disputes. Today in Africa, if there is a dispute, sometimes even a child can arbitrate. The African always looks for an arbitrator. It is part of his custom. If there is a dispute or a fight, the African looks around and says: Now, who's going to settle this thing? I've been in Africa and saw a man and woman fighting, they were arguing, not a physical fight, just an argument. The first time I didn't know what to do because this lady called me over and said, "I have won this argument and I'm tired of it. Come here, settle this thing." I didn't know what it was about or what I was supposed to do. She said, "Finish! Finish! I won the argument. Now settle it so that I can go on my way." She wasn't going to move until someone said it was settled. They thought that the Whites were just arbitrators but they did not know that the Whites would turn on them and put one against the other and conquer both of them. In many cases, this is what was done. Because of their African continuity, the slave revolts in the Caribbean Islands and South America were more successful. But there were slave revolts all over. When you say "maroons" most people think that you are talking about people in Jamaica. That's just a word for a runaway slave. There were maroons in the United States who ran to the hills and set up settlements and never submitted to slavery. All over South America there was a consistency in revolt in that there was a consistency in trying to maintain cultural continuity. In this country you will find the remains of African customs very plainly spelled out in parts of New Orleans. But New Orleans was under French rule and the French also bought in large lots and kept the lots together. You will find where people were permitted to settle without being sold and re-sold rapidly, they managed to hold themselves together.

Now, the purpose of this book itself: Why haven't we as a People, without asking foundations to do it, why haven't we set up a suitable memorial for the Africans who died in the Middle Passage? Why haven't we done it ourselves? We haven't done it in the past, why can't we do it now, although belatedly?. Why can't we also have a slave museum either adjacent to it or separate from it to preserve, so that our children will remember, the chains and the neck irons and the foot irons and the leg irons? This is what we came through and we are obligated never to let this happen again. First, we are obligated never to let it happen again to us. That is our first obligation and the world's obligation, after we take care of the first, is to join others of good will, if you can find them, to make sure that it never happens to anybody else in the whole world. But, don't take care of the world before you take care of your kith and kin, and don't apologize for giving preference to your case before you get on to other cases. What we have to do at this juncture in history is to locate ourselves on the map of human geography and shape ourselves for tomorrow so that we will be in a position that this will never happen again. We have to shake off and get rid of some of the naive attitudes we have toward ourselves, toward culture, toward words like "civilization," which is misused anyway, toward what we are going to have to do, toward people of our own group that we have misunderstood, toward concepts of nation and nation-management, toward where we are in the world, toward our national population and our international population.

We must take into consideration that in the West Indies, in South America, and in the United States there are easily 250 million African people. In the South Sea Islands, the Pacific Islands, and India and parts of Asia, maybe another 50 million. There are over 300 million Africans living outside of Africa. There are 500 million Africans in Africa. In the 21st century there will be a billion African people on the face of the earth. Where is our economy going to come from? If we built a shoe factory and made shoes for that many people our shoe factories would be running all night and all day! If we just think of serving each other, look what we can have. I'm saying that we have to start thinking "nation," thinking "alliances," the first alliance being with ourselves, because out of the Middle Passage and those who survived it came the making of a new civilization, a whole new way of life. If there are any people strong enough to have survived, they are strong enough to remake the world. If we can do this, we can do anything.

The one thing, in conclusion, that I'm asking you not to do is to forgive and forget. Your mission is to remember and to teach your children so that they can remember it. Because it happened to us, we have a special responsibility to ourselves to build a kind of humanity and partnership with all African people of the world that could serve as a role model for all of the people in the world. I'm not saying that we have to be nicer than other people in the goody-goody sense, I'm not talking about that at all, and I'm not talking about non-violence. I am saying we are fortunate because the entire continent of Africa, every inch of it, belongs to us. No matter who is there, who lives in Africa, all of it is ours, and we don't have to quote scriptures to prove it. We are the only people with a continent that belongs solely to us. Once you put African people, their energy and their imagination together, and once they begin to feed into each other and support each other there is no need for them to conquer anybody, or threaten anybody, and they, above all other people, can offer the world a whole new humanity and a new way of life. They might be the only people who can give this world some kind of security because they can see the utter stupidity of atomic weaponry because they want to live, and have proven it. I think the fools who are playing with it now also want to live, but they think they can use it and kill others and still live themselves. I think that bringing all these African people together will show the world that it would be a better place by virtue of them coming together and being successfully dependent upon themselves and delivering goods and services to themselves. They will improve not only the economy of the world, but the spirit of the world and the humanity of the world and the dignity of the world. But they will have to get some illusions out of their minds first. They have to develop an entirely different concept of education. Powerful people never educate you in how to take their power away from them, and their schools are not going to give you the kind of education you need. You have to make it, or take it. When you get the kind of education you need, you will discover the green fields of Africa and you won't have to go to Africa to improve Africa. Africa is where you are. You start with your community and with yourself and then you will begin to see and understand revolutionary change.

The greatest memorial that can be to the people of the Middle Passage, (while I call for and strongly suggest a physical memorial in addition to a museum of slavery, preserving the ornamentations, the chains, and atrocities so that our children will know that it wasn't easy), would be to remind them of the work they still have to do. I think that the greatest change is going to have to be with each one of you and your greatest memorial to those who died in the Middle Passage will be what each individual one of you does to bring revolutionary change to yourself and to your community. I think you should start with a mirror. You look into the mirror until you like what you see, and then you say: My revolution starts with me and my memorial to the people in the Middle Passage starts right now.

The End

NOTES ON REFERENCES

IN THIS QUINCENTENNIAL YEAR OF Christopher Columbus' encounter with the Indigenous People of the Caribbean Islands, mistakenly called "Indians," there is a proliferation of books on Christopher Columbus and his voyages that is tantamount to a small industry. The word "discovery," long used in relationship to his encounter, is at least being questioned. A few new scholars are bold enough to ask, "How can you discover something that wasn't lost in the first place?" In the preparation of this short account of Christopher Columbus and the African Holocaust, I have consulted a variety of books, new and old. In looking at the background to the atrocities set in motion by the Christopher Columbus Era, I have found two short accounts by Father Bartolomeo de las Casas most informative. They are *The Devastation of the Indies* and *The Tears of the Indians*.

Among Caribbean writers of African descent, the works of Eric Williams, the late prime minister of Trinidad and Tobago, were most valuable. His book, *Capitalism and Slavery*, written over 40 years ago is still a good source on how the slave trade was set in motion, especially in the Caribbean Islands. His last book, *The History of the Caribbeans: 1492-1969 From Columbus to Castro* is a good overview of slavery in the Caribbean Islands written for the layman.

Another small book on the subject written by Eric Williams in the late 30's, is *The Negro in the Caribbean*. His book *Documents on West Indian History, 1492-1655*, is the first of a projected four-volume work dealing with the relevant documents accentuating the history of the Caribbeans, its history and exploiters. In this book the use of the diary of Christopher Columbus is arranged in order to give the reader some insight into Christopher Columbus' thinking when he encountered the Indigenous People of the Caribbean Islands.

Among the new books on the subject that I found valuable is *Fulcrums of Change* by Jan Carew, (1988), *Columbus: His Enterprise, Exploding the Myth* by Hans Koning (1976), *The Black Holocaust, Global Genocide* by Del Jones (1992), "African Slave Trade, The Cruelest Commerce" an article in *National Geographic* by Colin Palmer (September 1992), *The Columbus Conspiracy* by Michael Bradley (1991), *Africa and the Discovery of America* by Leo Wiener (1992), *Slave Trade and Slavery* edited by John Henrik Clarke and Vincent Harding.

A note of acknowledgement of thanks toJack Felder for finding additional information relating to the slave trade and its aftermath that I otherwise would not have considered. I found his assistance most encouraging while I was preparing this book.

John Henrik Clarke

BIBLIOGRAPHY.

Africanus, Leo, *History and Description of Africa.*

Agbodeka, F. *The Rise of the Nation States: A History of the West African Peoples, 1600-1964.* London: Thomas Nelson and Sons, Ltd., 1965.

Akbar, Naim. *Chains & Images of Psychological Slavery.*

Alexander, Sadie T.M. *"Negro Women in Our Economic Life"* Opportunity July, 1930.

Aptheker, Herbert. *American Negro Slave Revolts.* N.Y.: International Publishers, 1963.

Aunt Sally, *Or The Cross, The Way of Freedom.* Cincinnati: American Reform Tract & Book Society, 1858.

Ayittey, George B.N. *Africa Betrayed.* St. Martin's Press, 1993.

Baldwin, James. *Going to Meet the Man.* N.Y.: Doubleday & Company, Inc., 1988.

Ballagh, James C. *A History of Slavery in Virginia.* Baltimore: Jonns Hopkins Press, 1902.

Barth, Heinrich. *Travels and Discoveries in North and Central Africa.* N.Y.: Harper Bros., 1857.

Bates, Daisy. *The Long Shadow of Little Rock: A Memoir.* N.Y.: David McKay, 1962.

ben-Jochannan, A. A. Josef. *From Afrikan Captives to Insane Slaves: The Need for Afrikan History in Solving the "Black" Mental Health Crisis in "America" and the World.* Richmond, Va.: Native Sun Publishers, 1993.

Bennett, Jr., Lerone. *Before the Mayflower.* Chicago: Johnson Publishing Co., 1975.

_____. *The Shaping of Black America.* Chicago: Johnson Publishing Co., 1975.

_____. *White Servitude in the United States.* Chicago: Ebony, 1975.

Blake, W. O. *The History of Slavery and the Slave Trade, Ancient and Modern.* Columbus: Osgod & Pearce, 1858.

Boahen, A. Adu. *"The Coming of the Europeans (c. 1440-1700)." The Horizon History of Africa.* N.Y.: McGraw Hill, 1971.

_____. *Topics in West African History.* Longmans, Green and Co., Ltd., 1969.

Bourne, E.G., ed. *The Northmen, Columbus and Cabot, 985-1503*. N.Y. 1906.

Bradley, Michael. *The Columbus Conspiracy*. Ontario: A & B Publishers Group, 1992.

_____. *The Iceman Inheritance: Prehistoric Sources of Western Man's Racism, Sexism and Aggression*. Toronto: Dorset Publishing Co., 1978.

_____. *Holy Grail Across the Atlantic*. Ontario: Hounslow Press.

Brathwaite, Kamau. *The Arrivants*.

_____. *Mother Poem*.

_____. *Sun Poem*.

_____. *X Self*.

_____. *Brazil: Mixture or Massacre: Essays on Genocide of Black People*.

Brent, Linda. *Incidents in the Life of a Slave Girl*. N.Y.: Harcourt Brace Jovanovich, 1973.

Brooks, Gwendolyn. "Why Negro Women Leave Home." *Negro Digest*, March, 1951.

Bruer, Hans. *Columbus Was Chinese: Discoveries and Inventions of the Far East*. N.Y.: Herder and Herder, 1972.

Budu-Acquah K. *Ghana, The Morning After*. Privately published in London.

Burroughs, Nannie H. "Black Women and Reform." *The Crisis*, 10 August, 1915.

The Louisiana Weekly, November 23, 1933.

"Not Color But Character." *The Voice of the Negro*, July, 1904.

Carew, Jan. *African Themes*: Northwestern University Studies in Honor of Gwendolen M. Carter. Ibrahim Abu-Lughod, ed. Program of African Studies, Northwestern University, Evanston, Ill. 1975.

Fulcrums of Change. 1988.

Carson, Clayborne. *In Struggle: SNCC and the Black Awakening of the 1960's*. Cambridge, Mass.: Harvard University Press, 1981.

Cash, Wilbur. *The Mind of the South*. N.Y.: Knopf, 1941.

Chamberlain, Alexander. *The Contribution of the Negro to Human Civilization*. 1911.

Cheatwood, Kiarri T-H. *The Butcher's Grand Ball: Meditations on Goree Island in Photographs and Carefully Chosen Words*. Richmond, Va.: Native Sun Publishers, 1993.

Chisholm, Shirley. *The Good Fight*. N.Y.: Harper & Row, 1973.

Claridge, W.W. *A History of the Gold Coast and Ashanti*. N.Y.: Barnes and Noble, Inc., 1964.

Clarke, John Henrik and Vincent Harding, eds. *Slave Trade and Slavery*. N.Y.: Holt Rinehart and Winston, Inc., 1970.

Cleaver, Eldridge. *Soul on Ice.* N.Y.: McGraw-Hill, 1968.

Cooper, Anna Julia. *A Voice of the South.* Xenia, Ohio: Aldine Printing House, 1892.

The Crisis, April, 1913.

September, 1942.

Cuthbert, Marion. "*Problems Facing Negro Young Women.*" Opportunity, February 2, 1936.

Danquah, Dr. Joseph B. *United West Africa (or African) at the Bar of the Family of Nations.* Privately published. 1927.

Dates, Janette L. and William Barlow, eds. *Split Image: African Americans in Mass Media.* 2nd edition. Howard University Press, 1993.

Davidson, Basil. *Africa in History.*

Black Mother: *The Years of the African Slave Trade: Precolonial History 1450-1850.* Boston: Little, Brown Co., 1961.

Davis, Angela. *Angela Davis: An Autobiography.* N.Y.: Random House, 1974.

_____. "*Reflections on the Black Woman's Role in the Community of Slaves.*" Black Scholar, December, 1971.

_____. *Women, Race & Class.* N.Y.: Random House, 1981.

deGraft-Johnson, J.C. African Glory.

de las Casas, Father Bartoleme. *The Devastation of the Indies: A Brief Account.*

_____. *The Devaluation of the Indies: A Brief Account.* English Translation. N.Y.: The Seabury Press, 1974.

_____. *The Disruption of the Indies.*

_____. *History of the Indies.*

_____. *The Tears of the Indians.* Translated by John Phillips. Academic Reprints. Stanford, Calif.

Drake, St. Clair. "*Why Men Leave Home.*" Negro Digest, April, 1950.

DuBois, Felix. *Timbuktu The Mysterious.* N.Y.: Negro Universities Press, 1969.

DuBois, W.E.B. *Darkwater: Voices from Within the Veil.* N.Y.: Schocken Books, 1920.

_____. *The Gift of Black Folk.* Boston: Stratford Press, 1924.

_____. *The Negro.* Oxford University Press, 1970.

_____. "*Segregation.*" The Crisis, January, 1934.

_____. "*Separation and Self-Respect.*" The Crisis, March, 1935.

Duster, Alfreda M. ed. *Crusade for Justice: The Autobiography of Ida B. Wells.* University of Chicago Press, 1970.

Ellison, Ralph. *Shadow and Act.* N.Y.: Signet Books, 1966.

Ely, Mike. *"The True Story of the Columbus Invasion."* Chicago: Revolutionary Worker, October 11, 1992.

Fage, J.D. *History of West Africa.*

Fanon, Frantz. *Black Skins, White Masks.* N.Y.: Grove Press, 1967.

Foreman, James. *The Making of Black Revolutionaries.* N.Y.: MacMillan, 1972.

Fosdick, Franklin. *"Is Intermarriage Wrecking the NAACP?"* Negro Digest, May, 1950.

Franklin, John Hope. *From Slavery to Freedom: A History of Negro Americans.* N.Y.: Random House, 1969.

Frazier, E. Franklin. *The Black Bourgeoisie: The Rise of a New Middle Class in the United States.* N.Y.: Collier Books, 1962.

_____. *The Negro Family in the United States.* University of Chicago Press, 1939.

French, Albert. *Billy.* N.Y.: Viking, 1993.

Gilbert, Olive. *Narrative of Sojourner Truth.* N.Y.: Arno Press, 1968.

Gilroy, Paul. *The Black Atlantic.* Cambridge, Mass. Harvard University Press, 1993.

Graves, Edward C. *The Invisible Chains.*

Gray, Thomas R. Recorder. *The Confessions of Nat Turner, October 31-November 11, 1831.* County of Southampton, Va.

Greene, Lorenzo Johnston. *The Negro in Colonial New England.* N.Y.: Atheneum, 1968.

Grier, William H. and Price M. Cobbs. *Black Rage.* N.Y.: Bantam, 1968.

Guerrero, Ed. Framing Blackness: *The African American Image in Film.* Philadelphia: Temple University Press, 1993.

Gwynne, James B., ed. *Malcolm X: Justice Seeker,* N.Y.: Steppingstones Press, 1993.

Hall, Jacquelyn Dowd. *Revolt Against Chivalry: Jessie Daniel Ames and the Women's Campaign Against Lynching.* Columbia University Press, 1979.

Hansberry, William Leo. *"Africa's Golden Past."* Part IV, Ebony Magazine. Chicago: Johnson Publishing Co., March, 1965.

Harper, Frances Ellen. *"Colored Women of America."* Englishwoman's Review, January 15, 1878.

_____. *Sketches of a Southern Life.* Phila: Ferguson Brothers, 1893.

Harrington, Oliver W. *Dark Laughter: The Satiric Art of Oliver W. Harrington.* University Press of Mississippi, 1993.

_____. *Why I Left America and Other Essays.* University Press of Mississippi,1993.

Hart, Albert Bushnell. *Slavery And Abolition, 1831-1841. 1906.*

Hedgeman, Anna Arnold. *The Trumpet Sounds: A Memoir Of Negro Leadership.* N.Y.: Holt, Rinehart & Winston, 1964.

Hernandez, Aileen. *"Ex-President of NOW Calls Group 'Racist'."* The San Diego Union, October 21,.1979.

_____. *"Small Change for Black Women."* Ms. magazine, August, 1974.

Hernton, Calvin. *"The Negro Male." The Black Male in America: Perspectives on His Status in Contemporary Society.* Doris Y. Wilkinson and Ronald Taylor, eds. Chicago: Nelson-Hall, 1977.

Herve, Julia *"Black Scholar Interviews Kathleen Cleaver."* Black Scholar, December, 1971.

Higginbotham, Jr., A Leon. *In the Matter of Color: Race and the American Legal Process, The Colonial Period.* N.Y.: Oxford University Press, 1978.

Hill, Robert B. *"Black Families in the 1970's." The State of Black America 1980.* The National Urban League, January 22, 1980.

Hines, Darlene. *"Female Slave Resistance: The Economics of Sex."* The Western Journal of Black Studies. Vol. 3, No. 2. Summer, 1979.

Hunton, Addie. *"Negro Womanhood Defended."* The Voice of the Negro, July, 1904.

Jackson, John G. *Introduction to African Civilizations.*

James, George G.M. *Stolen Legacy.*

Jairazbhoy, R.A. *Ancient Egyptians and Chinese in America.* Totowa, N.J.: Rowan and Littlefield, 1974.

Jones, Anna H. *"Woman Suffrage and Reform."* The Crisis 10, August, 1915.

Jones, Barbara A.P. *"Economic Status of Black Women."* The State of Black America. 1983. The National Urban League, January 19, 1983.

Jones, Del. *Black Holocaust: Global Genocide.* Phila.: Hikeka Press, Inc.,1992.

_____. *Culture Bandits. Vol. 1.* Phila.: Hikeka Press, 1992.

Jones, Landon Y. *Great Expectations: America and the Baby Boom Generation.* N.Y.: Ballantine Books, 1980.

July, R. *History of the African People.*

Kalifah, H. Khalif, ed. *The Campaign of Nat Turner.* Hampton, Va.: United Brothers Communications Systems, 1993.

Kemble, Frances Anne. *Journal of a Residence on a Georgian Plantation in 1838-1839.* N.Y.: New American Library, 1961.

The Koerner Report. 1968.

Koning, Hans. *Columbus: His Enterprise, Exploding the Myth.* 1976.

Kuhn, Alvin Boyd. *Shadow of the Third Century*. Elizabeth, N.J.: Academy Press, 1944.

Ladner, Joyce A. ed. *The Death of White Sociology*. N.Y.: Vintage Books, 1973.

_____. *Tomorrow's Tomorrow: The Black Woman*. Garden City, N.Y.: Doubleday, 1971.

Lash, Joseph P. Love. *Eleanor: Eleanor Roosevelt and Her Friends*. Garden City, N.Y.: Doubleday, 1982.

Lawrence, Harold G. *African Explorers of the New World*. N.Y.: Pamphlet, NAACP. Published July,1962. Reprinted in The Crisis.

Leakey, L.S.B. *The Progress and Evolution of Man in Africa*. London: Oxford University Press, 1961.

Lewis, David Levering. *W.E.B. DuBois: Biography of a Race 1868-1919*. N.Y.: Henry Holt, 1993.

Lewis, Ida. *"Conversation: Ida Lewis and Eleanor Holmes Norton."* Essence magazine, July, 1970.

Lomax, Louis. *The Negro Revolt*. N.Y.: Signet Books, 1962.

Lumumba, Chokwe, I. Obadele & N. Taifa. *Reparations, Yes!* 1992.

McDougald, Elise Johnson. *"The Double Task: The Struggle of Negro Women for Race and Sex Emancipation."* Survey Graphic, March, 1925.

Martin, Dr. Tony. *The Majority Press*, 1993.

Meier, August. *Negro Thought in America, 1880-1915*. Ann Arbor: University of Michigan, 1966.

Morrison, Crystal D. *Trial of Cristobal Colon*. Richmond, Va.: Native Sun Publishers, 1993.

Moss, Alfred A., Jr. *The American Negro Academy: Voice of the Talented Tenth*. Baton Rouge: Louisiana State University Press, 1981.

Navarrette, Jr. Ruben. *A Darker Shade of Crimson*. Bantam, 1993. New York Age, December 28, 1929.

Obadele, Imari A., Chokwe Lumumba & Kwame Afoh. *A Brief History of Black Struggle in America*. 1993.

Osler, Sir William. *Evolution of Modern Medicine*.

Ottley, Roi. *"What's Wrong with Negro Women?"* Negro Digest, December, 1950.

Owen, Chandler. *"Black Mammies."* The Messenger, April, 1923.

Palmer, Colin. *"The Cruelest Commerce, African Slave Trade."* Washington, D.C.: National Geographic. National Geographic Society, September, 1992.

Phillipson, D.W. *The Later Prehistory of Eastern and Southern Africa*. New York: Africana Publishing Co., 1977.

Polo, Marco. Travels of.

Pressman, Sonia. *"Job Discrimination and the Black Woman."* The Crisis, March, 1970.

Pullella, Phillip. *"Pope urges: Forgive white man for his injustices."* Daily Challenge. Bklyn, N.Y.: October 14, 1992.

Quarles, Benjamin. *Black Abolitionists.* London: Oxford University Press, 1969.

The Negro in the Making of America. N.Y.: Collier Books, 1964.

Raines, Howell. *My Soul Is Rested: Movement Days in the Deep South Remembered.* N.Y.: G.P. Putnam's Sons, 1977.

Reed, Ishmael. *Airing Dirty Linen.* 1993.

Rhodesia Herald, 1912.

Rodney King & The L.A. Rebellion, 13 Independent Writers. 1993.

Rodney, Walter. *How Europe Underdeveloped Africa.*

Rogers, J.A. *World's Great Men of Color. Vol. I.* N.Y.: Collier-MacMillan.

Rose, Willie Lee. *Slavery and Freedom.* N.Y.: Oxford University Press, 1982.

Salam, Yusef. A. *Capoeira: African Brazilian Karate.*

Schlesinger, Jr., Arthur. *The Disuniting of America.*

Schuyler, George S. *"Madame C.J. Walker."* The Messenger, July, 1924.

Scott, Emmett J. *Negro Migration During the War.* N.Y.: Arno and The New York Times, 1969.

Sellers, Cleveland with Robert Terrell. *The River of No Return: An Autobiography of a Black Militant and the Life and Death of SNCC.* N.Y.: William Morrow, 1973.

Shakur, Sanyika. *The Autobiography of an L.A. Gang Member.* Atlantic Monthly Press, 1993.

Sizemore, Barbara A. *"Sexism and the Black Male."* Black Scholar, March-April, 1973.

Smith, Elaine M. "Mary McLeod Bethune and the National Youth Administration." Clio Was a Woman: Studies in the History of American Women. Mabel B. Deutrick and Virginia C. Purdy, eds. Howard University Press, 1980.

Solanke, L. *United West Africa (or African) at the Bar of the Family of Nations.* London: The African Publication Society, 1969.

Staples, Robert. *"The Myth of the Black Matriarchy."* Black Scholar, November-December, 1981.

Sterling, Dorothy. *Black Foremothers,* Three Lives. N.Y.: The Feminist Press, 1979.

Stiddem, David R. *"It's Time We Rethink Our History."* Published in CALC Report, March 1990.

Still, William. *The Underground Railroad: A Record.* Phila.: People's Publishing Company, 1879.

Sweet, Nancy H. *Oh Africa, My Africa.*

Takaki, Ronald T. *Iron Cages: Race and Culture in 19th-Century America.* Seattle: University of Washington Press, 1979.

Terrell, Mary Church. *"The Justice of Woman Suffrage."* The Crisis 7, September, 1912.

Toynbee, Arnold. *A Study of History.*

Turner, Patricia A. *I Heard It Through the Grapevine.* Berkeley, University of California Press, 1993.

Vandercook, John. *Tom Tom.* N.Y. Harper Bros., 1926.

Van Sertima, Ivan, ed. *"African Presence in Early Europe."* Journal of African Civilizations Ltd. Inc. New Brunswick, N.J.: Transaction Books, 1985.

They Came Before Columbus: The African Presence in Ancient America. N.Y.: Random House, 1976.

Veney, Bethany. *The Narrative of Bethany Veney, A Slave Woman.* Worcester, Mass. 1889.

Wallace, Phyllis A. *Black Women in the Labor Force.* Cambridge, Mass. M.I.T. Press, 1980.

Washington, Mary Helen, ed. *Midnight Birds: Stories of Contemporary Black Women Writers.* Garden City, N.Y.: Doubleday, 1980.

Weatherwax, John M. *The Man Who Stole A Continent.* Los Angeles: Pamphlet, Bryant Foundation, 1963.

Wells-Barnett, Ida B. *On Lynchings.* N.Y.: Arno Press, 1969.

Welsing, F.C. *The Isis Papers.* Chicago: Third World Press, 1991.

West, Cornel. *Keeping Faith. Philosophy and Race in America.* N.Y.C.: Routledge, 1993.

Weiner, Leo. *Africa in the Discovery of America.* Innes & Sons, 1922. Bklyn, N.Y.: A & B. Publishers Group, 1992.

Williams, Chancellor. *The Destruction of African Civilization, Great Issues of a Race from 4500 B.C. to 2000 A.D.* Chicago: Third World Press, 1974.

Williams, Eric. *Capitalism and Slavery.* N.Y.: Capricorn Books, 1966.

_____ ed. *Documents of West Indian History, Vol. I. 1492-1655: From the Spanish Discovery to the British Conquest of Jamaica.* Port-of-Spain, Trinidad, W.I.: PNM Publishing Co., Ltd., 1963.

_____ *From Columbus to Castro: The History of the Caribbean: 1492-1969.* N.Y.: Vintage Books, 1984.

_____ *The Negro in the Caribbean.* N.Y.: Negro Universities Press, 1942.

Williams, Fannie Barrier. *"The Colored Girl."* The Voice of the Negro, June 1905.

"The Woman's Part in a Man's Business." The Voice of the Negro, November, 1904.

Wingfield, R.J. *The Story of Old Ghana, Melle and Songhai.* N.Y.: Cambridge University Press, 1957.

Woodson, Carter G. *The African Background Outlined.* New American Library, 1969.

African Heros and Heroines. Washington, D.C.: Associated Publishers, Inc., 1969.

INDEX